Pridh

A GUIDE TO
SURVIVING LIFE AS A MISTRESS

A GUIDE TO
SURVIVING LIFE AS A MISTRESS

Heather King and Jordan Hayes

ROBERT HALE · LONDON

© *Heather King and Jordan Hayes 1999*
First published in Great Britain 1999

ISBN 0 7090 5904 3

Robert Hale Limited
Clerkenwell House
Clerkenwell Green
London EC1R 0HT

The right of Heather King and Jordan Hayes to be identified
as authors of this work has been asserted by them
in accordance with the Copyright, Designs and
Patents Act 1988.

2 4 6 8 10 9 7 5 3 1

This book is dedicated to the two men without whom it would never
have been written – with our love.

Typeset in North Wales by
Derek Doyle & Associates, Mold, Flintshire.
Printed in Great Britain by
St Edmundsbury Press Limited, Bury St Edmunds
and bound by
WBC Book Manufacturers Limited, Bridgend.

Contents

Acknowledgements

Most of the contributors to this book want to remain anonymous for obvious reasons; nevertheless, they know who they are and we thank them sincerely for their candour and willingness to share their hopes, fears and dreams with us. We thank our partners for their support, despite their shock when they realized we were actually going to be published, and all our friends who have not only helped us through our bad times but have also encouraged us, proof-read our early drafts and given us invaluable feedback.

Jordan sends her love to her mother, who managed to hide her shock and then offered her support when discovering, not only that her only daughter was a mistress but also that she was going to share her experience with the reading public. She would also like to extend her warmest thanks to one lady in particular for her continuous encouragement.

Heather would like to thank her editor, who spent her holidays and any free time she could find in her busy schedule to read and re-read her work. She would also like to thank both her cousin and her brother for just being there.

We are particularly grateful to Michael Gouriet of Withers Solicitors for his invaluable legal advice in connection with the law relating to co-habitation in Chapter 8; but any errors are the authors' own.

Finally, we want to express our gratitude to our publisher, who took a chance on two hitherto unpublished women with a story to tell. His support, help and advice have been invaluable. Thanks to you all.

Introduction

This book is written by mistresses for mistresses and aims to help them to take a realistic view of their situations and offers some advice on how to cope with their affairs. It neither condones nor condemns extra-marital affairs, but recognizes that they do happen and will continue to happen. Although many books are written for married couples, very little is available for 'the other woman' and often she is ignored completely. When people talk about the pain of adultery, they rejoice if the marriage survives; few people ever wonder what happened to the third party, and even fewer care. We wonder and we care.

This is not an academic book: we have performed no national surveys and we are not trained psychologists. We have just talked to ordinary people with extraordinary stories to tell. We hope this book helps and informs you. It has not been easy to write. We have encountered issues we did not want to examine too closely and we have asked some questions we did not truly want answered. We have been told things we did not want to hear and have seen things about our relationships we did not want to see. Both our relationships have been affected as a result.

Each chapter is self-contained. Chapters 1 and 2 set the context by looking at the history of mistresses, views of society, cultural and demographic issues and extra-marital affairs in general before looking at the mistress's situation. Thereafter we have analysed the motivations and concerns of all the players and finally at the management of the relationship itself.

We felt it was important to look at the mistress' legal and financial position, and we have also included a chapter which contains statistics. During our research, we studied a number of surveys about extramarital affairs and infidelity but, unfortunately, the results are not consistent and lack information on mistresses. Therefore, rather than quoting selectively to prove a point, we decided that our interviews with over 150 people gave us much more accurate and detailed data than these surveys could provide.

Finally, we have included a number of case histories. Some of the mistresses we approached agreed to write their stories for us in their own words. They offer interesting insights into the ways these women coped with their situations – or not, as the case may be.

This has been a journey of discovery for both of us and we hope that, in some small way, it may either convince you to avoid being a mistress altogether or at least help you to take a realistic view of the affair and the ways in which you can manage your life within it.

Good luck to you all.

1 The Mistress: Definition and History

Most people around you would never suspect that you are a mistress and would be thoroughly surprised if they found out. In love with a married man, you will have felt in many ways you live outside 'normal' society and that even best friends, though sympathetic, are quick to point out the error of your ways. If you have called one of the few helplines available for mistresses, you will most likely have received the impression that you are in the wrong and were probably told that you lack self-confidence.

The popular press tends to publicize only women who are mistresses to known public figures; this, of course, is nothing new. If you belong to this group, it is likely that you are seen as having motives other than love, such as publicity-seeking or the promise of wealth and position. Rightly or wrongly, you are the stereotype mistress, and the public reads about it avidly and condemns it all, whilst maybe secretly wondering what it would be like to be you.

We will look at the dating game, mistresses through history and literature, and public figures of today. Society's views, cultural differences and new phenomena like Internet affairs will be discussed. Sex and love as well as other issues are debated and lastly, we give our definitions of adultery and infidelity, affair and fling in an attempt to discover, for example, whether a sexual relationship is required for adultery to take place and at what point an adulteress becomes a mistress.

British society has been established on principles of patriarchy and serial monogamy, and fidelity remains the goal for the majority of marriages. Yet while 80 per cent of the British regard extramarital sex as wrong,[1] one third would consider having an affair if the opportunity arose, and many do. Most people will know of at least one erring male in their circle of friends and family and many will have comforted a friend whose marriage has broken down because of an affair. The exact number of extramarital affairs taking place is extremely difficult to ascertain, since most studies into the subject are rarely based on any national probability samples. However, researchers estimate that between 25 per cent and 50 per cent of married men have affairs.

The question of how many mistresses there are is even harder to answer as most studies survey the married population, and we have been unable to find any statistics in the UK on single women having affairs. Moreover, the research that has been done is largely unreliable and no clear, universally accepted definition of a mistress exists. In order to interpret these figures within the context of this book and set the scene for the chapters that follow, we will explore what a mistress really is. This will include whether she is of a certain type, age or characteristic, and some of the reasons why she became a mistress.

Being a mistress is an aberration, a deviation from the normal or the typical. 'Normal' means to be married and have children. Around 75 per cent of women marry before they are thirty. Most start their marriage believing it will last, but nearly one in ten finds herself divorced around the age of thirty-five.[2] Single again, she is expected by friends and family to find a 'good man' and remarry, but the vast majority remain single long after the divorce. Only 6 per cent remarry within a year, although a further 15 per cent start living with a new partner.[3] This means that around 120,000 women each year have not found a new partner.

Most do not stay single by choice, and we need only to look at the increasing number of lonely hearts advertisements in newspapers or new introduction agencies claiming to give that 'very special service' to see that both women and men want a new relationship after divorce but have difficulty finding it. For most, it would seem, advertising is indeed the last resort and they have been disappointed many times. Sentences like 'No frogs, no beer bellies' abound. Reading between the lines it is clear that they have a good idea of what they want and that their criteria are probably more stringent than they were earlier on in their lives. By now they know what they like and will not settle for second best.

If there is a typical group of single women, who are potential mistresses, then divorcees fit the bill. Their independence will prove attractive to men who have status and power (the most common philanderers). They want to make a new life for themselves and remaining single until judgement day does not feature in the plans.

They might be over thirty-five but they are not ready to don the 'divorcee's weeds' or succumb to celibacy. But finding a suitable partner at this age is not easy, and getting to grips with being single again can be daunting, even for the strong-minded.

The divorcee is forced to enter a parallel universe, facing new challenges unprepared and unarmed. She has lived in a relationship for ten years on average, and suddenly, she loses her bearings and realizes she no longer knows her way around the dating game. There is a lot of inner searching for life's meaning and she finds that her married friends are behaving differently, even strangely, towards her. Just when she needs the support of her friends and the sociability of, say, a dinner party, the invitations dry up. When she is invited she will, more often than not, be asked if she could bring someone to make up the numbers, or worse, a blind date is organized for her with, inevitably, that beer-bellied, bald and boring ('but so nice') bachelor friend that her host takes pity on. She also finds that married men are quick to take advantage of the new woman on the scene. Somehow they feel she is fair game. Male friends she has known for years suddenly try to kiss her whilst showing her the house or getting her coat. Some will quite happily suggest that they should start a liaison ('I am happily married, she need never know'). One person in our research was recently accosted at a drinks party by a man (a reputable barrister) who suggested having sex with her. His wife was standing beside him. What she thought of the morality of this behaviour is anybody's guess, but she made a quick exit, feeling embarrassed and rather degraded.

The situation of the widow is similar to that of the divorcee. She is suddenly on her own, and while her immediate family and friends will be very sympathetic, she will face many of the same difficulties. She may have the added burden of financial problems, as she may not have been actively employed for some time, or the financial arrangements the couple had may not be adequate to enable her to continue her life as usual. She may, like the divorcee, also have children, which will make it more difficult for her to meet men outside working life, and work is where most affairs are initiated.

Women beyond their late thirties who have not been married are another group of potential reluctant mistresses. Some have realized that they are missing out and are ready fodder for the unfulfilled, unhappy or just exuberant married man. Some have remained single either through conscious choice or just because they never met a man they wanted to marry. Some are in a hurry for a white wedding with all the trappings, as their biological clock is ticking away, and others just want a happy, permanent relationship. Their plight mirrors the divorcees', with the exception that they are more used to being single. They don't want to get involved with a married man any more than the divorcees, but like her, they may fall in love with a married man and put their dreams on hold.

Single, younger women become mistresses, too, and this is often because older men seem more attractive than their contemporaries, because of their maturity, status and financial standing, although none of these need be foremost in their minds. As a rule, these relationships are short-lived, as younger women will usually be courted by a number of younger, unattached men, and, typically, unless the married man is willing to leave his wife she (the younger woman) will leave him.

After the sobering, often painful experience of divorce, the divorcee wants to find the right man and she is willing to wait for him. The widow may want to take even longer before getting back into circulation and in a way it is harder for her, as her relationship has been abruptly shattered, sometimes without any warning. The single woman will usually have had a number of boyfriends and lived with one or more, sometimes she has been practically married, albeit not within the law. So why do these three different categories of woman often become mistresses, how does it happen and is it love and companionship or just sex they are looking for?

The truth is, for any woman beyond her late thirties, the most attractive or eligible men are married. If she just wants to find *a* man, that is not difficult as there are enough around. But there is a real shortage of males to marry or to have a long-term relationship with, for very simple reasons. The mortality rates for men are higher than for women, divorced men have a higher propensity to remarry than divorced women (twice as many if over forty-five[4]) and men have a preference for younger women. Traditionally, women tend to 'marry up' and men 'marry down' in terms of education, earning power and age. The men who are available can therefore draw from a much wider range of potential partners than women, and the women who have the most difficulty are those with a higher education and beyond their late thirties.

American research into single women[5] shows that for every 223 unmarried women in their forties there are 100 unmarried men in the same age range, and that 90 per cent of highly educated, well-established men are married. For every ten women between forty and forty-nine with a college education that are only three single men who are older and better educated. The research also claims that the remaining single men tend to be least educated and the least well-off. Another statistic indicated by the survey is that 14 per cent of single men are gay against 4 per cent of single women.

In the future, it is likely that single women over the average marrying age who have never been involved with a married man will be in a minority.

For the woman over thirty-five, it gets more and more difficult to find a new relationship, as her circle of friends stays fairly constant and most people she knows are married. Liaisons with colleagues or clients are often ill-advised. Going out clubbing with a girlfriend no longer seems appropriate, whereas a play and a nice dinner does, and can be enjoyable, but rarely produces dates with interesting men. Introduction agencies charge anywhere between £100 and £4000 to supply a number of 'specially selected' contacts, and women who join them must fulfil their stringent requirements. Most agencies make it very clear that if the woman is size 16 or over (half of British women are),[6] she stands no chance. Ageism is rife. One agency states categorically that if your age group is forty-six to fifty, 'Life is getting harder, as of course gentlemen tend to date younger ladies, you are likely to have to request all the dates [sic]'; and if you're over fifty, the agency does not recommend its service at all, as 'gentlemen are getting thin on the ground as well as on the top'.[7] For men, the picture is different. For the age group of forty-two to sixty, the same company says, 'The older you get, the more in demand you become, tall interesting guys over 45 are usually spoilt for choice [sic]'.[8] *Vive la différence*, and tough luck if you are a female over forty-five!

Advertising produces various applicants in a process akin to an employment interview. The charges range from £5 in the local papers to £200 in the national newspapers for a small advertisement for two editions. Voicemail is popular, and can increase the cost by approximately £70 to £140. It leads to telephone conversations between people who have never met, with subsequent blind dates in pubs, cafés or restaurants. Some respondents are genuine, others are not, and many can be needy beyond belief. This is a game of chance. Many don't send letters or photographs and expect the woman to be gorgeous enough for the cover of *Vogue*. Some use voicemail options and practise heavy breathing, others keep harassing with endless letters, some are disillusioned with womankind and outright offensive, while some drive around after the date trying to find out where she lives. Advertising can work, but it is time-consuming, expensive, nerve-racking and it can be dangerous.

So when a woman is asked out by a man to whom she is attracted, she may say yes even though he's married. The last date she had may have been ages ago, and she may have considered that her only other options are to become celibate, a lesbian or to go out with uninteresting men. Whereas 99 per cent of married or cohabiting women have an active sex life, 39 per cent of unmarried women are celibate, along with 34 per cent of widowed, divorced or separated women.[9] She does not, of course, intend to become a mistress. She might just want to have a decent night out, with somebody who obviously appreciates her, and maybe have sex too. After all, she is only human. The married man will have his own justification. Most do not regard a one-night stand as adultery,[10] and for reasons explored in later chapters, he is out for some fun without responsibilities. The danger is not so much getting caught, but falling in love. As Carl Jung said, 'The meeting of two personalities is like the contact of two chemical substances; if there is any reaction, both are transformed.'

Sex and emotional love go hand in hand, and if the sexual chemistry works, both might find themselves hooked. Those who are courageous will just walk away as soon as they face the truth that he is married, but most women will reason that something must be wrong in his marriage if he is doing this. Many psychologists confirm this. Whether he is bored, sexually deprived or just married to the wrong woman seems inconsequential if he returns the love, as love usually requires two willing parties, and these women are no longer teenagers content with unrequited love. If she stays she becomes the mistress, usually involuntarily and unintentionally.

She is, in fact, a wife-in-waiting. If only she had met him before he got married, things would have been different. That is what they both say. She stays in the wings, sometimes for years, wishing and hoping that he would finally make a break. But there is always some obstacle. The wife is unwell, the children are too young, the grandparents too old. Whatever the excuse, the end result is that she stays a mistress. Statistics on affairs are at best confusing and misleading, but evidence suggests that around 20 per cent of married men divorce because of an affair[11] and only a fraction of those move in with their mistresses. Furthermore, unless the lover leaves his wife within the first year of the affair then he is unlikely to do so, ever.

So what keeps her there? Are these reluctant mistresses just desperate women who have given up hope of ever finding another man who would come close to what they have? The truth is simple. They are women of many backgrounds, social status, characteristics, looks and talents. Any one of us could be sitting in the office or in a café, sharing a table with a mistress and we would not know it. There is no standard pattern. The mistress did not intend to become a home-wrecker, she just wants her share of happiness in life – happiness to which she feels justified. She may be plump, she may be slim, she may be gorgeous or she may be plain, she may have a doctorate or she may have no qualifications, but she is loved. Maybe, because she does not take things for granted, she is more attentive to providing pleasure in the relationship, ignoring mud on the carpet, wet towels on the floor or bristles in the sink. There is simply no time to be bothered by such trivialities.

Married women who become mistresses are often unhappily married but unable to change their lives because they have become financially dependent over the course of a long relationship. The reasons for staying are often tangible enough. Many have married relatively young, left paid employment to bring up children and are used to a lifestyle which would be unaffordable if they divorced. It is difficult to say whether the unhappiness of these marriages is real or imagined, but something is obviously not right in their lives. The married mistress is in a very similar situation to that of her married lover; though perhaps genuinely in love, she also cares for her family. Alternatively she may be seeking a way out from her current marriage or just filling a gap in her life.

A recent survey by a women's magazine, compiled in association with Relate, stated that 66 per cent of married women had committed adultery and 24 per cent confessed to having had more than two liaisons. Many were incredulous at their own infidelity. 'I am no longer judgemental,' noted one of the respondents. 'I never believed that I could be capable of such an act. I'd had a strict moral upbringing and had strong family values.' For one in ten, the affair led to the breakdown of their marriage – 84 per cent of these said they had no regrets.

The word 'mistress' conjures up an image of a wanton woman in a short skirt, black suspenders and red nails: a young blonde bimbo chasing somebody else's husband. Media attention to mistresses of public figures enforces this stereotype, but in fact these 'modern courtesans' are very much in the minority. Love does not seem to be on their agenda; their motives are publicity, the promise of wealth and position. There is another type of wanton woman, the 'single-minded' individual who has grown to like her own independence so much that she prefers married men who do not require any commitment or threaten to mess up her lifestyle. The married mistress can sometimes fall into this category in the sense that she does not want her marriage threatened and feels safer with a married man. Her motives are sometimes very similar to those of resolutely married lovers.

In using the term 'modern courtesans' we mean women who choose their lovers based on purely mercenary motives. However, there is often a fine line between these women and anyone who selects a partner on the basis of potential income, connections and background. But in clear-cut terms, this type of wanton woman is often underprivileged in one way or another, lacking in education and stable background, but she is street-wise, straightforward and, in a rather American fashion, knows what she wants and goes for it.

Bienvenida Sokolow, 'Lady Buck', is quoted as saying: 'I longed for independence. But this meant money, more than I could ever earn. So I looked for men who'd made a fortune. Through these men I would make a fortune of my own.' The *Daily Mail* calls her a courtesan and a modern mistress in order to point out a contrast: rarely, these days, do lovers support their mistresses financially. However, these women are not always blonde bimbos or beautiful, their targets, after all, often being older men past their prime. Nevertheless she is ready to sell her story, when appropriate, to the highest bidder.

The single-minded wanton mistress is happy with her status. She can live her life as she pleases, she makes no compromises and is accountable only to herself. She can have the light on and read in bed as long as she likes. She can buy a pair of expensive designer shoes without provoking comments or curl up on the sofa in her pyjamas to watch her favourite video on a Sunday afternoon when *Grandstand* or *Rugby Special* is on. Having a permanent man would rather disturb all this, and married men are the kind of part-time lovers who fit into their busy schedule. They are there to carry the coal in as required and provide an easy relationship with no ties or demands.

These women have no scruples about dating married men for the simple reason that they believe that the man is responsible for breaking his vows. Unlike their modern courtesan counterparts, they are not in search of fame or fortune and they don't set out to catch married men. It has been suggested that these women have a 'chronic attraction to the unavailable', but the truth is probably that they find married men more relaxed, better lovers and less fuss than single men. These women love their independence and maintain emotional detachment; but inevitably, on occasion, they reluctantly fall in love.

History tells us of many famous mistresses. Several hereditary English peers are descendants of extra-marital relationships, often from centuries ago. One of the most famous such liaisons was that between the orange seller Nell Gwyn and King Charles II. Nell was not the only mistress Charles had. In fact he sired fifteen children by a number of women and gave titles to many of the offspring. The

current Duke of St Albans owes his title to Nell, who in 1684, threatened to throw her son out of the window unless Charles procured him
a title.

In those days it was expected for the upper classes, in particular, to
make good marriages for fortune and title, often arranged by parents,
and find love and sexual relationships elsewhere. You could say that all
parties were more or less happy with these arrangements. The class
structure worked marvellously to this end. A lowly girl of no means
like Nell could obtain the relatively highly envied and prestigious position of royal mistress. She would never have coveted the queen's position, since she would have accepted that her background ruled out
such privileges or opportunities. All she wanted was a good life and
better prospects for her son. Charles, on the other hand, got to frolic
as much as he liked, while the queen seems to have accepted that her
position was unassailable and her offspring would be heirs to the
throne.

Mistresses from those days seem to have had certain features that
were appreciated by the men they courted. They were deemed to have
honourable qualities, such as loyalty, style and sterling class and distin-
guished discretion. In the late nineteenth century Edward VII is said to
have chosen his mistresses with characteristic discrimination: Lillie
Langtry was luscious and witty, Alice Keppel seductive, shrewd, play-
ful and inoffensive. The Marquise de Pompadour, mistress to Louis
XV, who stayed in his court for twenty years, was described by Voltaire
on her death as having, 'la justesse dans l'esprit et de la justice dans le
coeur' (the soundness of judgement and fairness of the heart).

Today's media, when reporting on affairs and mistresses, are more
censorious. The royal admission of adultery by the Prince of Wales was
broadcast to millions of viewers, while Princess Diana's interview with
Martin Bashir on *Panorama* (November 1995) excited a frenzy of
tabloid interest. Interestingly, Camilla Parker Bowles seemed to exhibit
some of the old-fashioned values of a mistress, discretion and reliability, whilst Diana's lover, the army officer James Hewitt was mostly
seen as a cad. The Duchess of York's frolics with the toe-sucking financial adviser John Bryan were viewed as utterly beyond the pale. Tory
cabinet minister David Mellor's mistress, the actress Antonia de
Sanchez made comments that raised hairs on the neck of most
mistresses when she said, 'Women get involved with married men
because they don't want the domestic side of things.'

Literature has long recounted desperate love affairs which are
emotionally moving. Just think of novels like *Anna Karenina* and
Madame Bovary, films like *Casablanca* and *Brief Encounter* or plays

like Harold Pinter's *Betrayal*. What moves us, in the innumerable examples from art, is the idea of true love thwarted by convention or conscience. We accept that people can fall in love, even if they shouldn't, and it is hard for most of us to condemn Anna Karenina. We would have liked to see Dr Zhivago marry Lara. We accept that it is right for Humphrey Bogart to abandon Ingrid Bergman at Casablanca airport, but most of us wish they could have each other. After all, they are madly in love. It feels wrong and right at the same time, and very sad. The truth might be that only a few people actually experience true love, at least at the right time, and therefore idealize its fictional depiction, which mesmerizes them with its potent strength. As long as it doesn't happen on our own doorstep we cry our eyes out for the unhappy lovers having to return to their spouses.

Further afield, cultural differences abound. In 1988, when the Australian prime minister, Bob Hawke, crying and desolate, admitted to adultery on national television, the reaction of his countrymen, judging by next day's headlines, was to slap him on the back and say 'Good on you, Bob.' The British would have found this in very bad taste. The French are known for their tradition of '*cinq à sept*' ('five to seven', the times between which lovers meet); and France Telecom gained a certain notoriety when it decided to itemize only the first three digits of phone numbers in order to protect philandering spouses. 'Five to seven' affairs are apparently still a part of French culture, and the 'good' French wife, at least of the older generation, still continues to turn a blind eye. When President Mitterand was exposed as having had a long-established relationship with Anne Pingeot, resulting in a daughter, Mazarine, Mrs Mitterand allowed both of them to be present at his funeral in Jarnac in January 1996. Such magnanimity was unheard of, even in France. The younger French generation, however, is changing and finds it all a bit old-fashioned.

In the United States, in 1986, 34 million women were unmarried and one out of every five women had no partner. The number of single men in their forties was half that for single women. An American woman who divorces at thirty-five is statistically likely to remain single for the rest of her life. The singles scene is very active, and dating agencies are an established industry, whereas here they are just entering the growth phase. A new cult movement has sprung up in the United States, aiming to tell women how to get their man. Americans have always believed that it is possible to succeed in anything, providing you commit yourself, and marriage is no exception. Many books have been published on the rules of modern dating. These include: how to romance the man you love – *The Way He Wants You To!*;

dating and relating in middle life – *Dating: What He Said . . . What She Heard . . . What He Meant*; to sex and dating – *The Officially Correct Guide*; and love online – *A Practical Guide to Digital Dating*. A recent addition is *The Rules: Time Tested Secrets for Capturing the Heart of Mr Right*.

There are seminars, helplines and even Rules Watchers, on the lines of Weight Watchers, to support individuals in their quest. The content is generally rather old-fashioned and consists of playing hard to get, listening to your instincts and doing exactly the opposite. You come to appreciate Oscar Wilde's quip that there are only two great tragedies in life: not getting what you want and getting it. In that order. Grandmothers would thoroughly approve, but whether this approach would work with the British male has yet to be tested. One of the Rules' authors is quoted as saying, 'We Rules Girls end up with husbands. After years of getting it all wrong, I did the Rules, got married and now I am two months pregnant.' Dating courses also abound, some with tantalizing titles like 'How to Steal the Man You Want from the Arms of Another Woman.' It is all about manipulating the male – and not sleeping with him, even if you'd like to. It does seem very naive but, who knows, it is obviously working in America. Or are the women just so desperate and the men so gullible?

Politics are also changing the scene. The solemn Finns, after the collapse of the Berlin Wall in 1988 and the subsequent influx of Russians to Helsinki, find their main newspapers inundated with sex advertisements. Every restaurant and bar has its resident girls and opportunities for affairs have therefore greatly increased. What this will do to the mostly monogamous, steady Finnish male, and whether it will increase the divorce rate, are anybody's guess. The world and our values are slowly changing. The British still believe in marriage as an institution but only 25 per cent think it's for life. In 1993 the lowest ever number of marriages was recorded in England and Wales, and divorce rates rose to their highest level ever, 13.9 per 1,000 of the married population.

Those who want to stay in their marriages but want to have an affair as well have new ways of meeting their lover. Dating agencies catering for adulterers are on the increase. In Berlin, business is booming for Christa Appelt's agency, whose clients are married and fully intend to remain that way. She has some single women on her books who have careers, their own money and do not want to get married and have children. The married clients are respectable professionals – lawyers, doctors, academics and businessmen – who have a strong sense of duty towards their wives and children but who want to have a 'safe' extramarital relationship without complications. Most of the men say that their wives have lost interest in sex; some are bored and restless and just want to escape the mundanity of everyday married life.

Another phenomenon of today is cybersex, that is, affairs on the Internet. If you thought that physical sex obviously plays a crucial part in adulterous relationships, think again. According to Helen Fisher, author of *Anatomy of Love* and an anthropologist at Rutgers University in Newark, New Jersey, a cybersex attachment can be strong enough to be considered an affair, even if the parties never physically meet. Social scientists in the United States argue that a computer friendship easily graduates to an emotional affair when a) it becomes more intimate than your primary relationship, b) your real-life mate doesn't realize how deeply you have become involved, and c) there is a sexual tension, even if it is never acted upon. The first divorce cases are taking place in the United States today where cyber-sex adulterers are accused of sexually explicit affairs on the Net, even though there has been no actual physical contact.

The Oxford English Dictionary defines adultery as sexual inter-course by a married person with someone other than one's spouse. According to this definition, adultery takes place only if coitus occurs. If we look at the verb 'to adulterate', the meaning is given as 'to make inferior, impure, or adding a less valuable, harmful substance'. According to Christian law the sins are different depending on who commits them. Thus, the Church distinguishes between adultery – sexual intercourse between a spouse and a third party – and fornica-tion, in which an unmarried person has sexual intercourse with some-one who is married.[12] The Old Testament permits male infidelity with an unmarried woman but condemns as a capital crime adultery by a man with another wife or any near relatives.

Western societies operate on Judaeo-Christian moral principles, by which extramarital affairs are illicit and grounds for divorce. Other societies function differently, as testified by dozens of ethno-graphical studies. For example, out of 139 societies surveyed in the 1940s, 30 per cent permitted men and women to have extramarital affairs either during certain holidays or festivals, or with particular kinfolk, such as one's wife's sister or husband's brother, or under other special circumstances.[13] Among Inuit Eskimos, wife lending is customary and not considered to be adultery. Amazonian Kuikuru Indians have between four and twelve lovers and disappear regularly to the forest in the afternoons to engage in extramarital sex. Closer to home, in the villages of Central and Southern Italy extramarital affairs are part of everyday life, although they are conducted with discretion, not unlike the 'cinq à sept' tradition in France.

No society tolerates female adultery while punishing the male, and more cultures have restrictions on women than on men.[14] In Western cultures, moral standards are applied unequally between the sexes and double standards are rife. Women are no longer expected to stay virgins until marriage, but unwritten rules of behaviour apply. Pre-marital sex and cohabitation is largely accepted, but whereas a man is congratulated for his conquests, the woman who engages in sex at the first encounter or has a couple of boyfriends on the go is still considered sexually promiscuous. In a way it was easier for women in the 1940s and 1950s, where both sexes knew what the 'right' conduct was. Perhaps this is the reason for the American movement of Rules, although it does seem like a step back in time.

In the realm of affairs, it is the mistress who seems to bear the brunt of the blame. She is seen as the scarlet woman, the one who is misbehaving. A number of books have been written about extramarital affairs, and the mistress is usually dismissed with the term 'the other woman'. Their lovers are seen as victims, to be pitied for their weakness for female charms, and the wronged wife receives most of the sympathy. Morally, it must be conceded that the married man or woman who engage in extramarital sex are the ones in the wrong, as they both are breaking their marriage vows. The single mistress ought to be judged differently, because she is, after all, a free agent. In terms of blame, however, all parties must take their share: the married lover or the married mistress, because they both flout their marriage vows and hurt two people; the mistress, because she knows he is married and does nothing about it; the wife, because her marriage is suspect and she has not noticed, does not care or for whatever reason feels unable to do anything about it. Nevertheless, she must take responsibility for looking after her relationship.

Affairs, real or imagined, are amorous. They are about love, sex and friendship, though not necessarily in that order, between parties where as least one is married to or in a permanent relationship with somebody else. Whether physical sex alone counts as infidelity, or whether emotional love is sufficient to constitute adultery is probably irrelevant. Legally, consummation is still required for divorce proceedings on those grounds, but sex and emotion cannot easily be separated. One is rarely without the other, even if the sex happens through a sexually explicit correspondence, as recent developments in cyberspace testify.

Sex is the glue that binds relationships together. Robin K. Shymer says in his book *One Flesh – Separate Persons*, 'Sex is not everything, but it is a catalyst for many other things, and, since so many other things must be right for it to function well, also a touchstone for the quality of the total relationship.' D.H. Lawrence tells us that 'Where there is real sex there is an underlying passion for fidelity.' Ambrose Bierce defines love in his *Devil's Dictionary* as 'Temporary insanity cured by marriage,' and Oscar Wilde, with some artistic licence, comments that, 'There is nothing in the world like the devotion of a married man. It's a thing no married woman knows anything about.'

Some affairs go on for years, founding a fantasy on borrowed time, with both parties escaping the reality of everyday life. In that sense Antonia de Sanchez's comment, 'Women get involved with married men because they don't want the domestic side of things,' is correct, but it applies to both sides. Lovers can dismiss many of life's banalities from the equation. There are no arguments about the mother-in-law's visit, money, children's education, the weekend rugby trip or the girls' night out next week. Time is too precious, and the few evenings or lunch hours that the lovers have together are inevitably spent in renewing the relationship, one which never attains the normal state of a full-time relationship. This means that the infatuation stage can last considerably longer than it would under normal circumstances, thereby artificially extending a relationship that might otherwise fizzle out.

A fling can be described as a brief time of unrestrained pleasure and frivolous amusement in the sexual sphere. The difference between an affair and a fling is of course relative to the circumstances and the persons involved. When men are asked about infidelity, they generally do not count 'one-night stands' as affairs, whereas women do. Flings can be seen as aberrations, mental and/or physical, in which the parties choose not to let the liaison deepen to any real level of emotional involvement. Because sexual betrayal has occurred, they must count as extramarital relationships. It is of course nonsensical to impose a rule in which a fling becomes an affair after a set amount of time; what makes the difference is emotional involvement. Many affairs start as flings, in which both parties are just looking for pleasure to relieve daily pressures, a boring marriage or loneliness, and grow from there, a development often unintended by either party. Similarly, there are no exact time limits to becoming a mistress instead of having an affair. It is simply that the affair develops into a more permanent arrangement, a parallel marriage of a kind.

A mistress, according to the *Concise Oxford Dictionary*, is a 'Woman loved and courted by a man; illicitly occupying place of wife or having permanent illicit sexual relationship with a man.' Other definitions are similarly non-specific, and it is for this reason we felt it was necessary to make the distinction between reluctant and wanton mistresses, and have used these terms throughout the book. The former category represents the majority, women who never thought they would have an affair with a married man; and the latter describes one who sets out to do just that, or at least, does not mind the fact at all. There are grey areas, as with any definitions, but it is clear that the motivations of the two groups are quite distinct. The differences between the two are described more fully in Chapters 3 and 4.

All unmarried mistresses have one attribute in common: they are strong and independent, because they have to be. Otherwise, they could just get married. Getting a man is not difficult but finding the right man, with the right chemistry, is. They are brave enough to seize happiness when it's there and to live their lives alone instead of taking second best.

The impossible dilemma faced by the lover or the married mistress who falls in love with their partner in crime is well described in another quotation by Oscar Wilde: 'There are two great tragedies in life, losing the one you love and winning the one you love.'

2   Reasons for Extramarital Affairs

You are not the first, nor will you be the last, woman to fall in love with a married man. For some reason, the way you feel about him has made a mockery of both social and moral conventions. It would be wonderful if, following marriage, libidos magically become monogamous. Unfortunately, this is not the case, and when the attraction is strong enough, people turn into adulterers and fornicators despite what they hold true or what they have been brought up to believe.

Innumerable books have been written about sexual infidelity, each trying to pinpoint why it happens. In this chapter, we will consider this, but will also aim to turn the question on its head. We want to examine why extramarital affairs do *not* happen and, perhaps more importantly, why people marry in the first place. You might not like some of our answers, since, despite what you probably think or hope, love does not appear to conquer all.

Each mistress sustains a relationship with a married man. In order to explore some of the many reasons why he has decided to be unfaithful to his wife, we first need to look at marriage itself and its importance to our society and individuals.

Most heterosexual people expect to marry and this expectation is nurtured from an extremely early age. Society, the laws of the land and religion enforce and validate this aspiration and, as any single person will tell you, marriage is seen as the normal and accepted thing to do. When meeting someone aged forty or over who has never married, most people would wonder what was wrong with them or, especially if he is a man, whether he might be gay.

Marriage is regarded as the cornerstone of our society and marital breakdown is often blamed, in part, for the deterioration of collective morality. Surveys have examined the difficulties encountered by children of single parents and the greater likelihood that these children will pursue anti-social activities. However, on the issue of cause and effect it is difficult to isolate marriage breakdown from other factors such as environment, social class and education. It is not marriage itself that is significant but the maintenance of a loving and enduring relationship between two people. The fact that marriage exists at all might suggest that, unless they were tied by legal, moral and social rules, some would not or could not sustain such a relationship for any length of time. For such people, marriage becomes a constraint rather than the benefit it should and could be.

Few people question the desirability of marriage. People might ask the single person why they are not married but seldom ask husbands and wives why they did marry and if, with hindsight, they would do so again. We did ask and received some very interesting replies. In addition, we discovered that the success of a marriage is based more on compatible expectations than on any romantic notion of pairing for life.

The positive reasons that people give for marrying are that they are in love; they want to spend the rest of their lives with their partners; and they want to have children. The less altruistic reasons given are that they have reached the right age; are afraid of being left on the shelf; all their friends are married; and they want to get away from home. The more disturbing reasons are that they want their partner's money, status, or possessions. Most people believe that marriage will guarantee their particular requirements in some way or another. In fact, the only aspect of marriage supported by the law is the third. The success of the other factors depends solely on the people involved.

Whatever the reasons for forming the bond in the first place, marriage is sustained predominantly by the fact that both husband and wife believe that it is better to stay together than to be single. This could be because they are still in love or care deeply about each other and the thought of being apart is anathema to them. It also could be that there are children to maintain, that we live in a society that supports couples more than singles, or any number of less romantic reasons, such as pure inertia. For those who find themselves in a marriage that is not fundamentally based on love or strong affection, there is a greater likelihood that at some time in the future they will look for these qualities elsewhere.

Each marriage is unique. None the less it represents a way of life that has evolved over time so that two people can live together. Inevitably, compromises will have to be made and learning processes undergone wherein each person will strive to understand, accommodate and sometimes change their partner's requirements and way of life. This does not happen automatically; it takes time and work. Both participants, therefore, have to invest a good deal of understanding, tolerance and compromise in their relationship. If this investment is perceived to be too one-sided, the natural outcome is dissatisfaction.

The successful marriage can take many forms. Some partners spend twenty-four hours a day together, while others do not see each other for long periods. Some strive for equality for both in all things; others set clear demarcation lines and split responsibilities. Most assume sexual monogamy, whereas others support sexual freedom. Both husband and wife are trying to find a formula that works for them, for inside the marriage there really are no set rules. The only rules exist outside, in the world of convention, morality and law, and these can be, and often are, broken.

There are few truly bad marriages: those where one partner is abused, physically, emotionally or mentally; those where one partner is severely restricted by the other; those where communication has broken down irrevocably. Society does not seek to preserve such relationships but wants to see them either changed or abandoned. As for the rest, in the most part they work and do not adversely affect the people involved. They are at best life-enhancing and at worst bearable.

Marriage has been around for a long, long time and, despite the trends, will be around for a long time to come. It is mentioned in the Bible, documented in the Egyptian hieroglyphs and spoken of in the ancient texts of China. However, monogamy is a relatively new phenomenon and even now most of the cultures in the world are polygamous. Even the inhabitants of Britain were polygamous until monogamy was introduced, not by Christianity, as most people believe, but by the Romans.

This book is primarily aimed at people living in the West, where monogamy is the accepted norm and infidelity is seen as unacceptable and as grounds for divorce. But it is worth remembering that many cultures exist where neither of these two precepts apply. There are cultures where marriage can be ended easily and with no stigma attached, cultures where multiple partners are not only acceptable but encouraged and cultures where mistresses are recognized formally.

Marriage based upon love is relatively new, and still uncommon if we look at the world at large. The two most traditional reasons for marriage are the combining of assets and linking of families. Even as recently as the nineteenth century, people married for status and position and then looked for their love interest elsewhere.

Although mistresses have always existed, society's attitude to them has varied throughout the ages. Once it was seen as acceptable to have a mistress only if she was married. Now it is more usual for the mistress to be single. This has much to do with the greater independence afforded to women in the twentieth century – they can now maintain themselves rather than relying upon husbands to provide for them. This, as with most progress has proved to be a double-edged sword.

We cannot be sure whether men and women were meant to pair for life given that, these days, married life can be as long as sixty years or more. Nor can we know for sure whether the absence of marriage would cause the irretrievable breakdown of our society. It is also debatable whether at the age of twenty-seven (the average age for marriage) anyone can be absolutely sure that they have met the right person for life.

We are given a relatively short time-span in which to find our life partners. It is expected that, at some time between the ages of eighteen and thirty, most of us will find the person with whom we will be content to spend the rest of our lives. The pressure to fall in love, or at least get married, between these years is immense. Most people do find someone with whom to share their lives successfully. However, little allowance is made for the lovers who might not meet each other until they are in their forties or even fifties. Few, in fact, have the courage to wait that long. For this reason, some marry, not the love of their lives, but someone who is there at the appropriate time. A sobering quotation runs, 'Most people marry too young and for the wrong reasons but, if they are very lucky, they will never meet the one they should have waited for.' Many people who have affairs are 'unlucky'. Nevertheless, convention insists that, once the marriage vows have been taken, the union must be sustained at all costs.

In the marriage ceremony the future husband and wife make promises to each other that are intended to be kept for life. One of these is to love each other. This promise is potentially impossible to keep, since it involves an emotion over which none of us has complete control. Love cannot be made to endure, just as it cannot be forced to cease: everyone knows this, yet still the promise is made. Love can be feigned or suppressed, but it cannot be manufactured – nor destroyed – at will.

The likelihood of two people continuing to love each other with the same passion for life is slim, but, like the people themselves, the love can and, in most cases, does change. Inevitably, some couples will grow apart. It could be that they develop different interests, characteristics or ambitions. In these cases, the marriage might continue but it does so by force of convention or inertia rather than love and growth.

The birth of children can change the love focus from partner to offspring, which is one of the reasons why children become so important and can hold a marriage together. Children readily give and receive love. Nevertheless, most of us need both to love and to be loved in relationships that are more equal than those between parents and children. Where the parent–child bond becomes an overriding force within the marriage, it is likely that romantic love will be sought elsewhere.

Of the two sexes, women look for love within their relationship much more than men. A woman will stay with her husband, or leave her husband more readily, depending on where she finds that love. For most men, this is not the case. Even if love is found outside the marriage, it is seldom sufficient to cause most men to leave but it may persuade them to have affairs.

Recent experiments with monkeys have determined that males become bored with their partners after a time, and when a new female is introduced into the family circle, will quickly become 'unfaithful'. Meanwhile, his partner will seek to stay with the male she knows best. However, if after a time his first mate is reintroduced to the male, he will leave his 'mistress' to return to her. All he appears to want is variety, whereas the female wants stability. The scientists suggest that this indicates a generic tendency of males to be unfaithful, seeking originality and opportunities to impregnate multiple partners, whereas females tend to be faithful, looking for protection.

So perhaps infidelity for men and fidelity for women are actually programmed into our genes. This indeed makes some sense in terms of our survival as a species at a very basic level. Therefore, if this is the way we are determined to behave, it appears that society's rules are in conflict and should be changed to accommodate this genetic necessity. Conversely, perhaps one of the tasks of humankind is to strive to rise above any inherent animal behaviour, whatever the form, and not to use it as an excuse. Monkeys may help to explain male infidelity, but they do little to explain female infidelity.

Looking at animals for indications about our own behaviour is fraught with dangers. Few animals mate for life, many are sexually promiscuous and, commonly, males abandon females after mating. Males of many different species preside over harems, and some females actually devour their mates, usually during or immediately following intercourse.

Homo sapiens seems to have developed its own rules. Many are unfaithful to their partners, yet most marriages survive these infidelities. Some are damaged permanently but others are actually strengthened by the misdemeanour (not unlike our laboratory monkeys cited above).

The most common reasons given for infidelity are lack of companionship and/or incompatible sexual requirements within the marriage. The former is cited most often by women and the latter by men. People place most emphasis on the sexual element of affairs because it is based on physical acts; feelings cannot be so easily demonstrated, or, by extension, proven in a court of law.

Sex in the extra-marital affair will usually be different from sex within the marriage. The married party feels freer and will often indulge in more adventurous sex within the affair than they ever would with their spouses. There is something about the temporary release from responsibility and commitment that encourages freedom of action. An affair, whether we like it or not, is defined in terms of sex; a marriage is not.

The secretive nature of the extra-marital relationship afford the participants the opportunity to do things with their lovers that they would never dream of doing with their wives or husbands. This is not restricted just to sex but also covers codes of behaviour. In general, the lover is seldom aware of his mistress's deeper needs since he has little involvement in her day-to-day life and is not called upon to take responsibility for her well-being. Just as some people in cars behave with appallingly bad manners that they would never dare display in personal contacts, so the lover sometimes behaves badly when with his mistress. The secrecy, like the metal casing of a car, causes his behaviour to become more impersonal. The fact that these men can walk away from their mistresses (and do so repeatedly – normally to return home) is part of the relationship's attraction.

Sexual patterns are bound to change within any long-term relationship as needs and desires alter and the relationship matures. Some would even go as far as saying that it is inevitable that sex will play a smaller and smaller role as time goes by. Passion, they argue is replaced by less exciting but more stabilizing aspects of partnership, such as companionship and friendship.

A key point in most marriages is when a wife becomes a mother. This change of role often has the effect of subduing sexual appetites on both sides. Psychologists suggest that some men draw comparisons between their wives and their own mothers, thereby lessening the tendency to see them as sexual partners. Sometimes, women with children lose interest in sex altogether (and sometimes their husbands, too), as those children become the focus of their lives. Two of the most likely times for a husband to be unfaithful is when his wife is pregnant and in the year after the birth. This could be a direct result of the man's lack of sexual gratification during these times, but it could also be a reaction to the added responsibility and might even indicate jealousy towards the new arrival.

Trying to find men's true motivations for their infidelities is extremely difficult since they are far less likely to examine or question their behaviour than women. One has only to read the large number of women's magazines to realize that, from a very early age, women are encouraged to understand and analyse themselves. They fill in personality questionnaires and worry about their appearances, social lives and sexual performance. Men have few such magazines. Women are used to discussing their feelings and trying to understand their own, and their partners', motivations. Not so for men; in fact they will often see it as weakness to probe too deeply into personal feelings and to analyse motives. It is hardly surprising, therefore that they are also much more prone to self-delusion.

Men are also better at following rules, accepting the status quo and 'playing the game'. Women tend to be far more disruptive, preferring to ask why rather than accepting situations blindly. This might, in part, explain why most divorces are initiated by women and not by men – it is all a question of how deeply they perceive the reality of their situation. What is casual to a man, is not casual to a woman.

For the married woman, lack of closeness and communication with her husband makes her extremely vulnerable to infidelity. If she enters into an affair it is because it offers her what she feels she is missing from her marriage. Sex for her is part of the communication and closeness she seeks and is seldom the prime cause of the infidelity.

It is not uncommon for relationships between married couples to lose their edge over time. However, the decline of sexual activity is only significant in terms of what sex actually means to the husband and wife. The range covers everything from basic sexual relief to deep expression of love. It is a fact that sexual requirements, not fulfilled within the marriage, become a significant and very common trigger for infidelity and for the subsequent development of the affair.

However, despite the fact that it would somehow be more comforting, and make life simpler, if we could dismiss affairs as merely being triggered by sexual appetites, it is not always the case. This makes affairs appear less significant than they often are. Sexual attraction may explain why a particular adulterer chooses a particular partner but does not always explain why he/she was looking in the first place.

Several additional factors are known to cause spouses to stray. These include revenge, in those situations where a betrayed husband or wife might seek to get their own back or restore their self-esteem; mid-life crises, in which people start to feel old and want to reaffirm their attractiveness to the opposite sex; power, in which sexual conquest is used to boost self-image; an attempt to reassert individuality, in which, say, a woman feels lost in her role as wife and mother or a man senses his only role is to provide for his wife and family; and lastly there is serendipity, in which opportunity and attraction occur simultaneously.

Except for revenge and affairs within open marriages, it is difficult to assess how many of the above reasons are justifications after the event rather than the actual trigger. Even if these are valid reasons, there are still those marriages to which some or all of these apply yet the parties still remain faithful to each other. Therefore they cannot always be cited as the true causes of all extramarital affairs.

If, as a very conservative estimate, 30 per cent of married people admit to being unfaithful then 70 per cent are saying they are faithful. Even if we allow for the fact that many men do not consider one-night stands as infidelity, this still gives us a large sample to examine for further details. This group gives some interesting clues.

We asked a number of men who claimed they were faithful to their partners why they had never strayed. The three top reasons, in order, were that they were afraid of discovery, they loved their wives and they did not want to hurt their wives. All these answers were based upon a desire to maintain the marriage and the expectation that it would be damaged or destroyed by the affair. When questioned in more depth, most men admitted that, if they were sure of escaping detection, they probably would sleep with another woman if the opportunity arose. So does this mean that all adulterers think they can escape detection, that they do not love their wives, that they do not care if they hurt their wives and that they do not want to maintain their marriages? The answer, in an overwhelming number of cases, is 'no to most of the above'. The exception is the first.

Most adulterers do believe that they can escape detection or else know, or presume, that their partners would not react adversely or leave them if the affair was made known. The latter attitude, in nearly all cases, was expressed by those involved in open marriages. It was also cited by serial adulterers – those people who, having been detected before and having survived the ordeal, felt confident enough to stray again. The second most significant factor we identified was opportunity. Unless the couple can meet, which requires freedom, spare time and a suitable location, the affair is not going to happen. So, in summary, and at the most basic level, if the opportunity exists and the potential adulterer expects to get away with it, infidelity is extremely likely when an appropriate and willing partner is found.

Other reasons given to us for remaining faithful were fear of sexually transmitted disease, upbringing (for example, those having a strong moral belief or religious faith are much less likely to commit adultery) and commitment to either their immediate or extended family. One man, a rare exception, added the consideration that it would be unfair to the other woman as he would never ever leave his wife. Yet all these reasons are no less applicable to those men who become lovers – except perhaps the last, since most men, let alone lovers, do not appear to be quite so benevolent to the other woman. Therefore the answer we are seeking does not appear to lie here either. So we talked to the unfaithful for further clues.

Few of the lovers we spoke to, and even fewer mistresses, said they were actively looking for a relationship when they met their partners, but most lovers alleged that all was not well within their marriages – although since perfection in any relationship is extremely difficult, if not impossible, to attain, there will always be something missing from a marriage. What honestly triggers the affair is the fact that two people meet, they are attracted to one another and this attraction is strong enough to outweigh the married party's current commitment to his or her marriage. The stronger this commitment, the more powerful the attraction has to be. We also noted that the more intense the extramarital affair becomes, the more the married party tries to justify his/her actions.

Despite the risk it is surprising how many men have affairs with women who are known to their wives. This seems to add an extra level of spice to the relationship but will make the discovery doubly painful for their wives if they ever find out. But, as we mentioned previously, most lovers do not anticipate discovery and therefore seldom consider in detail the potential consequences of their actions.

If we accept that in most cases the affair provides something for the married party that he or she asserts cannot be found within the marriage, we must also admit that, whatever this missing piece is, it is seldom sufficiently important to cause the marriage to end. It appears that almost everyone works in one way or another to sustain their marriages, despite the problems, and for some an affair is merely one of the tools that can be used.

Some affairs do lead to marital breakdown, but the fact that fewer than 10 per cent of lovers then go on to marry their mistresses tells us that it is not simply a case of replacing one wife with another. Most men see an affair as an addition to the marriage; most women see the possibility of a future husband. This fundamental difference causes most of the problems and is particularly marked in those affairs where both parties are married. The woman is more likely to be prepared to leave her husband than the man is to leave his wife, no matter how intense the affair becomes. Often she does not discover this basic difference in attitudes until it is too late. Only if both share the same view of the relationship does the affair prove to be mutually satisfying.

There are also those people – more commonly, men – who just enjoy having affairs, usually for the sexual variety, but few are honest enough to admit it. They may use the excuse of deficiencies within the marriage, but the truth is normally different. For some, the exploit gives them the illusion of freedom, making them feel less trapped by their marriage. They can play at being independent whilst maintaining the security of their dependent relationship with their wives. Others find personal intimacy difficult and they can avoid this with both wife and mistress by being partially committed to both. Some simply enjoy the chase and the conquest, whereas others, usually those who have been married a long time or are finding marriage too predictable, are seeking to enhance their sex lives or bolster their self-esteem. In the latter situation, marriage is usually helped by the venture. In all cases, no matter what the motivation, having a mistress is invariably a boost to the man's ego. It makes him feel more confident and more virile and he takes reassurance from the fact that he can still attract the opposite sex.

In an affair, the married man always wants to set boundaries, even though he thrives on the diversion, excitement and forbidden nature of the relationship. Most will establish, at the earliest possible opportunity, the fact that they do not intend to abandon their marriages. Fear of losing or hurting their children is the most commonly used excuse. Their mistresses accept these excuses willingly in most cases. They want to believe that theirs is an example of true love and are comforted by the notion that their lovers would be with them if only circumstances were different. This is easier than confronting the possibility that their lovers do not want to be with them permanently, certainly have no intention of leaving their wives and probably do not love them in the way they want to be loved.

Marriage involves a number of relationships, not just that between husband and wife. These serve to enforce the man's personal commitment. They include those with the children of the union, those with parents, colleagues and friends. Marriage involves the expectations of society, rules (both written and unwritten) and the roles he defines for himself within these. Each additional relationship framing the marriage represents another bond, and the more bonds that exist the more likely that the marriage will endure.

If we were trying to define the characteristics of a man who was more likely to leave his marriage for a new love, we would have to cite a great number of factors. If he has no children or they are grown up, if his parents are dead or if he does not have a good relationship with them, if he has a low public profile, if he has a tenuous or non-existent relationship with his wife's family, if he is an only child or is not close to his siblings, if he has been married for a short period of time or an extremely long period of time, if his wife is being unfaithful, if he has no religious beliefs, if most of his friends are divorced or single – then he might, only might, be more likely to walk away from his marriage. Yet, even then, it is an extremely difficult thing to do and almost everything in his personal and social life works to enforce the state of matrimony and oppose divorce. He knows this and his head will remind him constantly of this reality no matter how great the temptation of another woman might be. Divorce just does not make sense to him, at any level.

Infidelity is not just the domain of married men, although statistics seem to indicate that unfaithful married women are in the minority. Our two basic requirements of an affair – confidence and opportunity – may help to explain why. Typically women have less confidence than men and most do not have the same kinds of opportunity to have affairs, although working wives do have more opportunity than those at home with children. Women are more likely to be disappointed by their marriages than men. They have far more romantic notions about marriage and often make more personal sacrifices throughout, especially when children are involved. It is still more likely that women will abandon their careers than men, and they often miss the resultant lack of stimulation. The fact that the marriage then becomes the focal point for their lives means that they look within it for more of their personal fulfilment than their husbands do.

Married women, more than married men, are likely to be precipitated into an affair as a direct response to some problem within their marriages. They are more aware of their husbands throughout and are more concerned about detection, unless they are using the affair as a way to signal problems in the marriage. They often feel a greater need to assert themselves as people in their own right, and the lover who can make them feel special, listened to and attractive again has found a winning formula. Many husbands are notorious for not praising their wives, for missing those special dates and for presuming that their wives know that they love them. In these cases, the reassuring, outward signs of love are missing. The majority of married women who enter into affairs do so because the man they meet makes them feel special and because they believe themselves to be in love. Few will risk their marriages for sex alone and do not enter into an affair lightly. They, more than their male counterparts, are likely to become involved seriously in the affair and it therefore presents a greater threat to their marriages.

Some married women have affairs with single men, but this book is primarily written for those women who become involved with married men, which is a more common occurrence. Despite this, it is worth mentioning that a married woman is far more likely to leave her husband for her single lover than a married man is to leave his wife for his mistress. This has much to do with the different way in which the sexes view the potential of the extramarital affair.

The woman who enters into an affair is usually looking, at least at the beginning, for more than her lover is, and this is amplified when the woman is single. The married mistress still shares many of the problems with the single mistress, but her situation is different in a number of ways. These differences are highlighted in Chapter 6.

However, in most situations these days, the man is married and the woman single. He already has a support structure and attendant relationship at home, she does not. Her need for personal intimacy is therefore greater than his, no matter how difficult his home life may be. He has human contact and a diversion when he returns home. She has her thoughts, a good book or a cat. It is hard to understand why any woman, looking at the situation dispassionately, would enter into such a relationship given the foundation from which it begins. However, in order for there to be such an affair, there must be willing, unattached women around who will accept their lovers' initial propositions. Why do they do it?

Single women are obviously not seeking revenge or a way to plug the gaps in their marriages. Nor are they trying to escape a relationship. They may be trying to preserve their independence by having a relationship without commitment or they may be looking for excitement without the monotony of day-to-day cohabitation. They may be looking for a way to improve their prospects by sleeping with someone who can offer them money, status, or both. Certainly, this is the popular perspective and most publicized view of mistresses, and such women do exist. However, most mistresses do not fall into this category. Whatever their reasons for initiating the relationship, and most do so because of a powerful initial attraction to their partners, they ultimately stay because they fall in love. The relationship is unfair to them; it often leaves them unfulfilled and lonely; it is punishing and often plain hard work.

It is believed that only someone with low self-esteem would continue to accept such a situation for any length of time, but most mistresses do not see it that way. They believe they have found someone special and regard low self-esteem as being prepared to accept second-best or staying in a relationship only because of the fear of being alone. To endure the situation, a mistress must have considerable courage and strength. Love, on its own, will not be enough if she is to sustain the relationship for any length of time. Few women have either the patience or the stamina to become long-term mistresses.

A true mistress is the woman who, knowing in her heart of hearts that she is extremely unlikely ever to become his wife, is prepared to accept an alternative role in his life. That does not mean she will stop dreaming, but it does mean that she has stopped deluding herself about an idealistic outcome. To a great extent, this type of mistress presents less of a threat to the marriage than an affair in which the woman might still be trying to break up her lover's marriage. However, few wives would accept this distinction, except perhaps in countries such as France, where people seem better able to understand the specific differences between the two roles. In some situations, it is probable that the man would have married the woman who eventually becomes his mistress had he been free when he met her – such is the depth of the relationship. This relationship, once established, begins to run in parallel to the marriage and subsequently takes on a completely different form and operates within different dynamics to his marriage. Both marriage and affair start from the same basis but they develop differently.

An extramarital affair, by definition, occurs outside a marriage but will seldom replace that marriage. It is initiated by an attraction, at any number of levels, between two people. It is sustained, or not, by the way in which that attraction develops. No matter how intense affairs become, they are seldom the true cause of marital breakdown, even if detected. Those who learn of their partners' infidelities do not have to see them as signalling the end of their marriages. Much depends on their ability to understand and forgive the transgression and whether they believe they can eventually heal the anger, pain, sense of betrayal and loss of trust they experience.

In most cases, those having affairs are not looking for a way out of their marriages, but for something to enhance their lives in one way or another. Absolutely no one is immune to temptation and no marriage will ever provide everything that an individual requires from a relationship. Whether the marriage is supplemented by the husband's relationship with a mistress, or not, ultimately depends upon his confidence, his wife's ignorance or acceptance and his mistress's resilience.

No excuse, no matter how seemingly altruistic or romantic, will be accepted for infidelity. The overwhelming directive from society is for each of us to preserve marriage irrespective of whether it represents a genuine love-match between husband and wife. This is true even if one of the partners finds love elsewhere. It is not love that is protected but marriage itself.

In the end, all we can say is that extramarital affairs are a triumph of feelings, no matter how base, over thinking. This is what makes them so difficult to justify. Whereas the maintenance of many marriages represents a triumph of thinking over feeling. We are all trained from an early age with varying degrees of success, to dismiss emotions in favour of rationality. It is believed that this is for the greater good. The twentieth-century morality of valuing thought over emotion is enforced by the very structure of our laws, relationships and society itself. Strong powers of thought are applauded, strong emotions decried. When asked, adulterers most often rationalize their reasons for staying married but can seldom rationalize their affairs in the same way. This, given the way society is structured, only serves to enforce the former and diminish the latter.

The act of marriage, often undertaken at an early age, asks us to make promises on behalf of our feelings and, at the very least, force them to remain constant, pointing in one direction for life. This, in most cases, seems to be an impossible promise to keep.

3   The Reluctant Mistress

The motivations of the married man who enters into an affair are complex, but, in this chapter, we are concerned only with the mistress's motivation. Whatever got you into this relationship, whether love, lust, excitement or even pure recklessness, it was strong enough to overcome the fact that your lover was already married to someone else. It is therefore unlikely that any amount of reasoning, no matter how logical, will change your feelings significantly. However, we hope at least to help you take a realistic view of your situation, think about your dreams and assess for yourself the likelihood of them ever coming true.

The reluctant mistress never wanted or intended to be a mistress, but has accepted her situation simply to be with the man she loves – a man who, for whatever reason, has decided not to leave his wife. A momentous battle has been fought between her heart and her head, with the heart being the overwhelming victor. To be a mistress, even in the 1990s, is socially unacceptable; it means an isolated lifestyle, with long periods of loneliness and lack of true fulfilment. She shares the man she loves with someone else – his wife – who holds all the cards and is given almost total support by society, the law of the land and every agony aunt in the world.

For such a mistress, each day is a state of limbo in which whole sections of her life and her lover's life are not shared. Each time she sees him is special; there are few 'normal' evenings when, for example, she does her knitting and he does the crossword or fixes the leaking tap. Time is too precious to waste on the mundane, and it is this, not the reluctance of the mistress to indulge in these activities, that marks the affair as so different.

For the same reason, the preciousness of time, neither party can be totally honest – spoiling the evening with arguments or bad feelings is pointless when there is quite simply never enough time to put things right again. Inevitably, then, so much that could be said is left unsaid and feelings are bottled up inside.

It is important to appreciate how much each mistress has to exercise self-control within the affair. Sometimes this control is a stated requirement from the lover, but, most often, it is a self-imposed discipline that will cause her to curb her most natural behaviour. If she truly cares about her lover, she will not want to compromise him in any way. This would not only threaten him but would also threaten their relationship. As a result, feelings of frustration inevitably build, as she cannot show her affection in public, must avoid being seen in certain places and must wait before being allowed to talk to him. The mistress learns, very early on in her relationship, that she is effectively on her own. This is one of the most painful burdens she has to bear.

The lover spends most evenings, weekends, holidays and often his mistress's birthday with his wife and family while she waits forlornly for the telephone to ring, trying meanwhile to occupy her mind with diversions. She cannot contact him when she wants to, nor can she control when or if she sees him.

This all seems to paint an extremely dark picture, yet it is common for most, if not all, mistresses; many soldier on, nevertheless. The love they bear these men is sometimes so great that nothing else matters. On the other hand, problem pages tell us that the mistress lacks self-esteem or that in some way her childhood is to blame. Invariably, the mistress will be told that either she or her life is deficient in some way. In order to understand the situation more clearly, the relationship must be explored from the very day it begins.

All relationships start in the same way. A spark of attraction, be it mental, emotional or physical, occurs between two people; sometimes the feeling has built over time, sometimes it is instantaneous. However, the woman must come to terms with the fact that her potential partner is married. Sometimes she knows he is married at the outset, sometimes not. This attraction is more common than most people are prepared to admit, but, at this point some people walk away and some do not. The mistress did not walk away and nor did her lover; only she and he know the true reasons. For her, almost without fail, it was an emotional rather than an intellectual decision.

There will never be an easier time to stop the relationship than at this point, and most people would cite the fact that the man is married as ample reason. However, all mistresses talk about the strength of this initial attraction, a strength that manages to overcome social convention, potential danger and the fundamental immorality of the situation. At this time all the inevitable problems are a million miles away and there seems no real reason to resist the temptation other than the relatively minor questions of social condemnation.

The man is married – fact. Both parties try to rationalize the situation before the relationship can proceed. The man normally explains why he wants to initiate the affair in terms of his wife and his relationship with her. He wants to justify his actions to the woman he is approaching and to set limits for any ensuing relationship. The mistress will rationalize why she will go ahead despite the fact that he is married – but often only to herself. We can be reasonably sure, however, that he has thought this through much more than she has.

In the beginning, it is highly unlikely that they are in love. Although love at first sight is a known and accepted phenomenon, very few of the mistresses we spoke to claimed this had happened to them. Instead they spoke of the fact that they had found someone who fascinated them, someone they wanted to get to know better; their thoughts were overwhelmingly in the present, the long-term implications never further from their minds. The lack of foresight is astounding in itself, and the best advice we can give mistresses at this stage is: think, for goodness sake, *think*! Often, from the outset, the mistresses' feelings simply took over, and although this is not a good excuse for initiating a relationship it is the only one most of them have.

Each mistress we have spoken to said that they thought about their lover's wife but not in any great depth. Some empathized with her as a woman and could identify with how she might feel if the infidelity were discovered, but very few considered themselves a threat to his wife or marriage at this stage; but nor did they consider that the wife would be a threat to them – both considerable oversights.

Throughout the relationship the wife, though occasionally brought into the conversation by the lover, remains a shadowy figure. The mistress falls in love with the man, not the fact that he is married. When composing a list of ideal characteristics for a partner, we can be sure that 'married' is seldom one of them. But no matter how much we might believe that our ideal is single, six feet tall with black hair and blue eyes, this does not stop us falling in love with a married five foot, bald, myope.

There is no lack of publicity on extramarital affairs, so no one can pretend that they were completely blind to the pitfalls. Yet each mistress feels that it could not happen to her, that somehow her situation will be different. At the beginning, the majority never thought it could or would get serious enough to cause any problems, either to their lovers or themselves. The case histories chapter gives some insight into the thoughts that mistresses had when initiating the relationship. Some are touchingly naive, others sound cold and calculating, but all fell well short of the reality.

We were interested in understanding how each mistress managed to rationalize to herself starting an affair, given that it is generally seen to be neither an advisable nor acceptable course of action to take. In answer to our questions, we received a number of common responses, which we list below, along with our assessments.

'There must be something wrong with his marriage, despite what he says, or he would not want me'
Here the mistress has inferred that the marriage is in trouble and that perhaps the lover is looking for something new or better. The marriage could indeed be experiencing difficulties; infidelity is often a symptom of some form of communication breakdown in the lover's relationship with his wife; but the situation is unlikely to be so simple. No marriage is perfect, and there will always be problems to overcome. Just because something is wrong, it does not follow that it is bad enough to cause him to walk away. Most marriages have their positive aspects too, and in the end it is the balance that matters.

'He would not risk his marriage unless he was serious'
His marriage might be at risk if he was serious, but at the outset most men do not believe that the affair will be any more than a temporary fling. Statistics show that the chances of a marriage breaking up simply because of an adulterous liaison are relatively small compared with other factors. He believes he will get away with it providing that his wife does not find out and he does not get too involved; at this stage, he is probably right. However, if the relationship with his mistress deepens, he might then find that his marriage is in jeopardy when he finds it increasingly difficult to walk away from the affair. So the risk is a long-term rather than a short-term consideration for him.

'I'm not hurting anybody'
O that this were true, but it is a dream rather than a reality. Perhaps the three people involved can escape damage in the early stages, but if the relationship has any longevity at all, someone is going to get hurt. What the mistress does not consider at this stage is that she will almost certainly end up hurting herself.

'I don't care what it costs'
The need to love and be loved is overpowering – there is nothing like it. You do not care if you die tomorrow; whatever it costs, you want

to live for the moment. You have not lived if you have not loved, and you may think that perhaps it will never happen again. While all this may be true, the costs can be great and the mistress may not be able to afford the emotional price she will be called upon to pay. In extreme cases, mistresses have killed themselves when they could no longer cope with the mounting problems.

On the other hand, the relationship can also be an experience or even a way of life to be treasured despite everything. Time spent with someone you truly care about is a time of great richness, and we have met few mistresses who have significant regrets about their relationships with their lovers or the price they had to pay. Initially, however, no one can truly know what the costs will be and therefore 'don't care what it costs' is often uttered in blissful ignorance of what is to come. At each stage, the relationship must be reassessed – 'Is this really worth it?' – and only the mistress can supply the answer. The key must lie in the amount of self-knowledge that the mistress has and an understanding of what she can afford. She can be assured, however, that no matter how deep her feelings may be, there will always be a price to pay.

'I can control/handle this'

At the beginning both parties believe this to be true, and until the relationship deepens and becomes established control of some kind may be possible. However, when in love, neither will be able to control the situation and, more importantly, neither is likely to want to.

'This will give me freedom'

A 'no-strings' relationship can sound extremely attractive. In theory, because the lover is married he will have little effect on the rest of the mistress's life. She might believe that she can go out with other men, decide what she does and does not do, effectively manage her own life. She is a modern woman, in control of her own life and with nobody to answer to. She can sleep late, not cook dinner if she chooses and call her lover for company whenever she wants.

This might sound idyllic, but in practice the story is often altogether different. Most mistresses end up being monogamous, the disruptive nature and intensity of her relationship often precluding the formation of a romantic bond with anyone else. The necessary spontaneity of the meetings also has an uncanny habit of playing havoc with her social life.

Of course, single life has its advantages, just as married life does; but those advantages are significantly different in a number of ways.

The absence of her lover becomes like a double-edged sword: on the one hand a kind of freedom, but on the other a lack of support and someone to care for her. The key problem for the mistress, as she will soon realize, is that she cannot see her lover when she wants. In this she has no freedom at all.

Sooner or later, he will begin to control when and where they meet, and as she loses this fundamental control so too does she relinquish most of her freedom to act unless she is an extraordinarily resolute individual. This means fitting him in to her busy schedule when she can; not cancelling previous arrangements if he calls and, of course, *never* staying in hoping the telephone will ring. We would like to hear from you if you are the mistress who has managed to achieve all this.

'He's not like other married men'
– and, naturally it follows that he will behave so much better than the rest of them. Of course. It is extraordinary how many married men make this claim – a claim that each mistress longs to believe but this is often self-delusion. For, although it is true that everyone is unique human behaviour is remarkably similar. Each mistress hopes that her lover is different, that the pitfalls that befall other mistresses cannot happen to her. While this is conceivably true, it is surely wise to assume he will behave like the vast majority until proven otherwise. This means that he is unlikely to leave his wife, he will demand control of the relationship and will not be there for the mistress when she needs him. That said, we recognize that as infatuation takes hold, everyone, whether male or female, will see what they want to see.

'He is married; I am not'
Roughly translated, the reasoning is as follows. He is intending to be unfaithful to his wife, his wife is his responsibility and the repercussions, as far as his marriage are concerned, are therefore also his responsibility. The mistress, on the other hand, is being unfaithful to no one, she has made no promises and is therefore free to act. If anyone should be avoiding this relationship, it should be the lover.

The logic may be sound but, nevertheless, the mistress will still be called to account by society and will often be held responsible for the effect of the relationship on her lover's wife and his marriage. This general attitude is based on two notions. First, that the husband belongs to his wife in some way and is being 'stolen' and, second, that he was not strong enough to resist temptation and therefore the mistress should have acted for him. In the former case, we believe that no one 'belongs' to anyone else whether married to them or not; and in the latter case we dispute the idea that the man is granted the get-out clause of 'weakness' while the mistress is not. But despite the injustice, when it comes to apportioning blame, no amount of logic will save her.

'How can this be wrong when it feels so right?'
We have left this statement until last, as we feel it needs to be examined in depth. Philosophers have been debating this fundamental question for millennia and have still not reached any universal conclusions. We cannot hope to cover all the ethical angles, but the above quotation is one of the most common cries we have heard and thus demands a searching enquiry.

Behind the statement lies the entire moral code the mistress has been brought up to believe in and which will eventually be used against her. If she has a religious belief, it is likely that her religion says it is wrong; her parents have told her it is wrong; society tells her it is wrong; and, in some countries, the law tells her it is wrong. Everything and everyone tells her it is wrong to have a relationship with a married man and, until she met him, she probably thought it was wrong too. It is this, more than any other, reason why the mistress is often seen as lacking self-esteem – deep down inside she feels that she is doing something bad and she gives this some, if not total, credence.

So many mistresses told us that they used to say 'I would never go out with a married man' and each of them believed this to be true. Yet something happened that overrode, and caused them to question, a basic morality that most people accept at face value. That something was simply, a feeling called love. Perhaps then, they are asking 'Why is love wrong?' – a question which we believe is unanswerable.

The element of a relationship that takes it beyond friendship between a man and a woman is sex. The term 'mistress', at least in common usage, necessarily entails a sexual element, and we therefore consider the consummation of the relationship to be a significant act and the first qualification of the mistress–lover bond. This helps to explain why most mistresses are single and most married lovers in jobs that give them freedom of movement. The former supplies the place and the latter the opportunity. Senior managers and politicians, who have more control over how and where they spend their time, and those whose jobs involve travel, have long been seen as the 'types' of men who have affairs. They are, but only by virtue of the opportunities their circumstances afford. It is interesting and sobering to consider how many more extramarital relationships would be established if men and women had less restrictive home lives and/or careers.

Looking back with hindsight, most mistresses see the consummation as the first form of commitment to their lovers, despite the fact that at the time none thought about what would happen next. Until she has sex with her lover the potential mistress is relatively safe, but, having done the deed, she can be cited in a divorce, pilloried by society and stoned in the Middle East for adultery; she has taken her first real step towards becoming a mistress in the eyes of the world.

Few of these thoughts are likely to have crossed her mind at the time. Although everyone acknowledges the presence of some form of risk, the type or degree of risk, and how it is perceived, varies from person to person. Perhaps the greatest risk is for the married woman, especially if she is not part of an open marriage. In this one act, she puts her marriage on the line. She presumes that this is also the same for her lover, but this is seldom the case. The lover's reasoning is sometimes significantly at odds with what we would expect it to be.

An interesting paradox is that the mistress's lover is, by definition, allowed to be unfaithful to her – he can also make love to his wife. This is likely to continue throughout the relationship and, although seldom a problem in the early stages, it will become an increasingly difficult fact to deal with later on. The lover might say that it happens very rarely or that he no longer has sex with his wife or that it is really of no consequence, and the mistress will be expected to accept the situation.

Unlike his wife, the mistress has no right to ask him to stop, no matter how much she might want to, and the lover will expect her to know this. She is aware that he sleeps with two women and the image is not an easy one to expel from her mind. The fact that the male lover appears to be able to maintain the two relationships with apparent ease also causes her considerable confusion, especially as he usually expects his mistress (and his wife for that matter!) to be monogamous. She assumes that sex is as significant to him, in terms of emotional commitment, as it is to her, but this is rarely the case. In the end, most mistresses try not to dwell on his marital sex life, certainly do not ask for any details and pretend it is not happening at all.

For those who have never had affairs, sex is often viewed as the focal point, the reason for the infidelity, the central motivation. For those seeking only physical gratification this is undoubtedly true, but in the enduring relationship between mistress and lover, it forms only part of the bond. Sex is part of love and love a part of sex. In this respect it is no different from the sexual bond in marriage.

At the beginning neither party will be sure whether the relationship has any future. It could just turn out to be a short fling that is almost entirely sexual, temporary and lacking any ongoing commitment. The end can be disappointing in many ways, especially if one or other party had hoped for it to continue, but the pain is seldom terminal and most people survive without too much trouble. However, if the meetings continue, a deeper relationship begins to form. The early days of the affair are without doubt exciting. Lack of time causes an artificial intensity as so much is packed into moments rather than days. Both mistress and lover are infatuated with each other and the times they are apart are spent thinking about each other almost incessantly.

Most meetings are arranged on the spur of the moment and normally at the lover's instigation, since it is he, not she, whose movements are restricted. The mundane aspects of life are all but abandoned as discreet venues are visited and the lovers plan interesting ways to spend their time together. But as time goes by, the fact that the man is married becomes increasingly significant. As the mistress watches her lover leave, each time knowing where he is going, she will spend more time considering the implications of the affair than she ever did at the beginning. She wonders how much he really cares for her and when she will see him again. She wonders whether his wife will find out or not and, if she does, what will happen. She looks for ways to fill her time and gives herself stern lectures about not letting this man run her life . . . until he calls again and she breaks yet another trip out with a girlfriend.

She starts drawing charts or keeping records of how much time he spends with her. Though the 'occupancy' ratio is seldom more than 10 to 15 per cent he occupies her waking thoughts almost 100 per cent of the time. During the first year she has actually spent only about one month with him, she has seldom seen him at weekends if at all, she has waited for him to return after family holidays and she has faced Christmas without him. Her family are starting to ask questions and she cannot take him home to meet her parents. Her best friend's eyes glaze over every time she mentions his name and she will bore anyone who will listen to her about her situation. Unless she is married, she is living as a single woman, not as part of a social partnership. All events and situations requiring a partner present difficulties for her since it is probable that her lover will not want to be displayed publicly.

She has discovered that he is not so easy to contact, and, slowly but surely, the affair passes out of her control into his. He seems happy with the way things are; she, increasingly, is not. Finally she realizes that this is not a good situation to be in – something that everyone who cares about her has probably been telling her since the affair began.

She wants more, she wants changes. She writes letters she will never send and starts composing poetry (often bad poetry) for the first time. She practises the conversations she will have and the points she intends to make and feels strong and brave – until he walks through her door again. In her head, she rehearses leaving him a hundred times while examining her emotions to see if she can cope; and a few, a very few, actually manage to say goodbye. The rest have now reached the point of no return: they are in love.

The realizations afforded the mistress in the first year point unremittingly to ending the affair unless her lover will leave his wife. The solution is blissfully simple: she should ask him to leave and if he says no then she should end the relationship. That last sentence was so easy to write, but it appears to be extremely difficult to do. Many mistresses do not even ask the question; those that do ask are then faced with deciding what to do with the answer. But whether the question is actually asked or not, there comes a point in the relationship when it is clear that the lover does not intend to leave his wife no matter what he might have implied or said to the contrary. This is an extremely common situation.

Most married men who are going to leave their wives for their mistresses leave relatively early on in the relationship – usually within the first six months. The exceptions are few and far between. If he does leave, the title 'mistress' mysteriously disappears and is replaced by girlfriend, fiancée or, eventually, even wife. The mistress is damned only by her lover's absence – his presence magically legitimizes her. However, it is more likely that he will leave his mistress if he feels that his marriage is at risk or, if not, want to keep both wife and mistress indefinitely. If the mistress concedes to the latter situation, she has now truly earned the title 'mistress': an implicit or explicit acceptance (no matter how reluctant) of the status quo.

By staying, she has made a significant and major conscious compromise. She knows what she wants (her 'top line') but is obviously prepared to settle for less, sometimes much less. At this stage, and indeed throughout the relationship, we advise her to consider just how little she would be prepared to accept before leaving him (her 'bottom line'). While the top line varies very little from mistress to mistress the bottom line is often greatly different, and it is this that helps to define the nature of the relationship that will be formed.

Why has the mistress decided to stay in a relationship that does not give her what she wants? The one thing that keeps her there is hope. Despite what her lover says, despite all the evidence to the contrary, she believes that if she loves him enough he might eventually choose her. Perhaps her lover is in love with her; perhaps he is not. If the former is true, then she cannot understand why he does not leave his wife; if the latter, she cannot understand why she will not leave him. All that can be said is that, whatever the situation, the pain of losing him is greater than the pain of staying. She has forfeited the option of not being hurt, so she chooses what hurts least.

The patterns of the relationship become established. Invisible demarcation lines are drawn that relate to what she can and cannot do. The lovers meet with some regularity and usually for similar lengths of time. Perhaps she calls him every morning or he calls her once a week or she waits and he calls her when the mood takes him. The relationship has no set content; each one is different. It can be based solely on lunchtime meetings or contain occasional holidays away together. But, whatever it consists of, there is obviously enough to keep both parties together.

The lovers become comfortable with each other, learning how to humour, how to comfort; what gives pleasure, what pain. They have long conversations about their interests and the male lover will often discuss things with his mistress that he keeps from his wife. Perhaps he feels that with the greater sense of freedom accorded him by the affair comes also a greater opportunity for self-expression. The lovers start supporting each other as in any other relationship; they become friends, good friends. Friends and lovers, but still only for 10 to 15 per cent of their lives.

At first the mistress may be happy. Something tangible has been created, she misses him when he is not there but she also knows she is going to see him again and some of her insecurity fades. This alone keeps her going. It feels settled and organized. Some mistress/lover relationships can and do last for years and years. These relationships become like parallel marriages, sometimes even stronger than the legal marriage by virtue of the kind of bond formed between mistress and lover. There are few obligations, possessions or even shared events to cement the two people together; the most significant components are the two people themselves – together simply because they want to be together. This can be one of the most special feelings in the world.

One of the best-publicized examples in recent years concerns Spencer Tracy and Katharine Hepburn, who were lovers for twenty years until Spencer Tracy died. She nursed him through his drinking bouts, they travelled together and had a great respect for each other. In the beginning Katharine Hepburn wanted to marry Spencer Tracy but he would not leave his wife and later, when he finally proposed, she refused him. Marriage was probably by then irrelevant. Prince

Charles's relationship with Camilla Parker Bowles lasted through both their marriages. Whatever the nature of this relationship, it was sufficiently strong to hold them together despite considerable cost to them both. On the other hand, the ten-year affair between Tim Rice and Elaine Paige, which attracted a lot of publicity, was finally ended by Elaine Paige when the pain of being a mistress became too great. In the eighteenth century, Byron's mistress stabbed his hand with a knife when he sent her away, probably for somebody else.

History is rife with affairs, mistresses and lovers, and so is fiction. Infidelity is not uncommon, as most people like to think, it is just well hidden by the vast majority of participants. This is predominately because society refuses to countenance its validity under any circumstances. Long-term affairs are not necessarily sordid nor are they confined to the rich and famous, as popular opinion would suggest. Though ultimately destined to fail in the vast majority of cases they can create extraordinary, loving relationships between two ordinary people.

Mistresses come extremely low on the list when it comes to sympathy votes. They are often held solely responsible for extramarital relationships and are accused of breaking up marriages. Yet our research has shown that, rather than breaking up marriages, mistresses often hold them together and make them bearable by supplying what is missing. The mistress is a symptom not a cause of difficulties in a marriage yet she, perhaps more than any other, bears most of the blame and most of the shame. True, she is not blameless but she does not deserve to shoulder most of the responsibility and stigma for a relationship formed by two people.

Instances of the 'kept woman' still exist but these are extremely rare. The mistresses we interviewed were not supported either financially or, for that matter, emotionally by their lovers and, almost without fail, what they did was out of love, no matter how misplaced or ill-advised. The majority live on their own, trying to manage their lives in extraordinary circumstances.

Being a mistress is not for the faint-hearted. Given the choice, most mistresses who have finally ended their relationships state they would never do it again. One of the key lessons learned is that any relationship requires significantly more give and take than a relationship with a married man allows. Such relationships are governed almost entirely by what the lover is prepared to give, and no one should settle for such an inequitable state of affairs – it is not wrong to need and ask for more.

However, despite the pain and frustration, nearly all mistresses still express some form of affection for their former lovers and many are still in touch with them as friends; a few are still in love with them. For those mistresses still in their relationships, their lovers are special, very special, and, although they spoke of the costs, all considered them to be worth it. None wanted to leave the relationship but most thought they ought to. The battle between heart and head, it appears, never ever stops.

But for most it's a sad, sad situation. Perhaps the response given by one mistress to the following question says it all: 'Why, when you found out he was married, didn't you walk away?' Her answer: 'Next time, I will.'

4 The 'Wanton Mistress'

You are a woman who does not mind that your lover is married to somebody else; you might even prefer it. Whether you have become a wanton mistress by conscious choice or by quirk of fate, you are happy with your situation, at least for the present. Your reasons are varied: you might feel that you have no choice, you might fear commitment or might simply be seeking your fortune. You may have been a reluctant mistress, abandoned your hopes and learnt to live with a relationship that is going nowhere. Or perhaps you are just bored and not prepared to settle for a single man who falls below you ideal.

You may be looking to marry your lover as a straight business deal, not believing in love or lasting romance. The fact that you would be breaking up a marriage is irrelevant to you. Alternatively, you may be married yourself and looking for sexual release and possibly friendship to complement a stable, but partly unsatisfactory, relationship.

Whatever the case, you feel you are in control of your emotions and your life. This may be true, for now, but life is rarely static, and you may be well advised to consider your future situation. This chapter looks at the different types of wanton mistresses and their motives, circumstances and prospects. It also attempts to make sense of the wanton mistress to her counterpart, the reluctant mistress.

We discuss the role and meaning of love, the quality that is often regarded as distinguishing whether the mistress is wanton or reluctant.

The wanton mistress represents the stereotype beloved by the popular press, yet although reliable statistics can be found, she is probably in the minority. She is often seen as cold, calculating and self-centred. This judgement might often be plausible on the surface, but there may be underlying reasons for her behaviour. The reluctant mistress will generally view her wanton counterpart as one who doesn't love her man, but this may not always be true. We all have our views of what love is and our own style of loving. There is no right or wrong way to love somebody.

Most of us will have found that the love we feel for different partners varies and that our experience of love with one partner changes with time. We also find it difficult to relate to others' perspectives or understand why we love a particular person. Despite extensive research on the psychology of attachment and love since the 1950s, researchers seem to face similar problems: it is impossible to tell whether being in love is based on reality, deception or a combination of the two; whether love is an attitude, an emotion or a set of behaviours; whether we should also look to brain chemistry of consciousness or further to mental state, emotional stability, childhood experiences or even demographic constraints like shortage of men available to women past the age of thirty.

The science of love is still in its infancy, offering a number of different approaches and theories with little common vocabulary. Most researchers agree that they still don't know what love really is, but many interesting and thought-provoking categorizations and ideas have been put forward: a recurring distinction is made between passionate, romantic and conjugal or companionate love. Passionate love involves a strong sexual base; romantic love is more focused on idealization of the other than on the sexuality of the other. Both types of love are intense and occur fairly early in the relationship. Companionate love has been defined as involving friendship and understanding, a concern for the other's welfare.

Zick Rubin[1] found that love is made up of four components: needing, caring, trust and tolerance. His research showed that every individual had their own concept of love, with varying amounts of each component. Liking or friendship was very different from love, although it often accompanied love, and respect was essential for liking but not for love. Sex was part of the need component and he also found that a sexual relationship can exist in the absence of the other components of love. Other researchers have come up with similar categorizations, usually based on the three behavioural systems of attachment, care-giving and sexuality.

A series of books have also highlighted the painful and negative side of love which could explain some of the feelings mistresses experience in their relationships. Stanton Peele likened love to addiction, where the relationship is necessary to the person's functioning and, like drug addiction, is difficult to escape. A possible theory for the survival of long-term extramarital love affairs could be that the lover has become dependent on the mistress for emotional security and, as their relationship never becomes habitual, their love remains at the passionate stage. As addictive love is marked by its exclusively inward, possessive focus, this would explain why so many lovers insist that the mistress is faithful to him and are often jealous of her 'other life'. Some researchers see jealousy as a hallmark of real love, but it has also been noted that 'jealousy goes along with both a sense of dependence on a relationship and with a person's feeling that he or she is in some way lacking'[2]. V. Adams adds that 'Jealousy is born of feeling that we have so little to give compared to someone else.'

While Helen Fisher's vocabulary is slightly different, the basic tenet of the three types of love remains. The research helps to explain some of the complexities of love and why a mistress may stay in a relationship for years, unable to make the break. It might also explain how it is possible to love two people at the same time and why our love experiences vary; but it still doesn't tell us what love is, nor can we draw any conclusions on whether wanton mistresses love their lovers. We must conclude that love is as we find it and experience it; we are all different and we cannot judge others' experiences by our own standards.

If we dismiss love as the major issue that differentiates the two types of mistress and concentrate instead on motives and circumstances, we can start to make sense of the wanton mistress. The key factor distinguishing her from the reluctant mistress is that she does not care that her lover is married. Indeed, marriage is rarely on her agenda, at least not with him. We have divided wanton mistresses into two groups, the modern courtesan and the single-minded mistress. Though not necessarily a clear distinction, it is a convenient starting point for understanding the wanton mistress.

The modern courtesan comes closest to the common stereotype. She goes after the man she has deliberately chosen, based on apparently mercenary motives. The man she selects is usually married and a good deal older, often a person in the public eye. Members of Parliament are prime candidates. This type of mistress is difficult to sympathize with, as she often perpetuates the cold and predatory image by giving interviews and selling her story to the newspapers.

The above encapsulates the generalizations usually made. Before we condemn her completely, we need to look beyond what she does to herself and others, considering her likely circumstances and the reasons she acts in this way. Her objectives seem clear enough. She wants to have a higher status in life, feel powerful and superior to her peers. She wants to be financially secure and able to live a lifestyle to which she has aspired but rarely been accustomed. She does not seem to care how she gets there or whom she hurts in the process.

She is likely to be disillusioned with life and what she feels it offers her. She may be the product of an unhappy childhood. While this might sound like a cliché, research indicates that people who have not loved or been loved in their childhood, may be unable to form loving relationships later in life and become 'affectionless characters'.[3] It is possible she has never been cared for and feels that she owes nothing to the world, waking up in her late twenties with a vengeance to correct the sense of injustice she feels.

The modern courtesan lacks self-confidence and is therefore unwilling or unable to seek work or study in order to achieve her ambitions. Whether intelligent or stupid, she is probably not well educated, for whatever reason, and therefore has not got the wherewithal or drive to change her life through her own endeavours. Her family background may be quite humble or, conversely, she may be a drop-out from an established, well-to-do family. Somewhere along the line however, she has acquired the taste of the good life.

She is overly jealous of other women who have 'made it', in her eyes those who are part of high society. She wants to show them she is better and more entitled to be there than they are. She may have been greatly disappointed in an earlier love affair, or perhaps she really was in love but was jilted for the sake of another woman who could offer her lover better status and financial prospects. She might be a victim of sexual abuse, which could explain why she is apparently satisfied with a man sometimes thirty years older – a man who can hardly provide her with mental compatibility or a satisfactory sexual relationship. Perhaps she has never experienced love or enjoyed sex, and therefore does not know what she is missing.

She will justify her actions as an unavoidable means of survival. If the man is fool enough to believe she is in love with him and that she has no other motives, then so be it. If he is able to betray his wife and endanger his public position, that is his problem, not hers. If his wife is not capable of keeping him, then he is for the taking. This type of mistress is often good-looking and attractive to men. 'Why shouldn't I make most of the assets that I have', she asks 'and besides, what is the difference between what I am doing and what women do who are on the look-out for marriages to men with good prospects?' In terms of the purely mercenary outlook, she might have a point.

Some women will marry for money and are prepared to exchange love for a fat bank account and all the associated trimmings. The latest research by Demos, the independent think-tank, shows more women today are selecting their partners based on their financial prospects,

ambition and drive, rather than their looks, age or attractiveness. Most
women think about marriage purely for money at some point, believing that they will escape poverty for good and live a luxurious life that
would otherwise be unsuitable. As divorce statistics soar and job security becomes a thing of the past, they prioritize comfort, hoping that a
kind of partnership or love will develop later. It might.

Statistically, the arranged marriages favoured by many other
cultures survive as well as or better than marriages founded on love.
The flipside, of course, is that most women in our society would find
it difficult to endure, let alone enjoy, sex with a man to whom they are
not attracted. Money does not always compensate for the lack of real
affection and intimacy, and many women who take this route end up
wishing they had made different choices. Some make a success out of
these marriages, regarding them as pure business contracts, mergers
between two individuals who share the same beliefs and pool their
resources in order to get what they both want.

The modern courtesan's thinking is on these lines, but she goes one
step further and simply chooses a man who fits the bill, whether he's
available or not. Sometimes the very fact that he isn't is preferable,
since she may be looking to use his married status as a lever for financial gain. Whatever her particular motives and reasoning, she has come
to believe that this is the only way she can get where she wants to be.
She has convinced herself that she never wanted a traditional marriage
anyway. This is, of course, exactly what she would have wanted, but it
just never worked out. Having suffered enough hardship and mental
anxiety over her financial circumstances, she has decided to protect
nobody's interests but her own. She needs to be looked after for once.

She might not set out to destroy her prey, but she will use him to
gain contacts to secure her future prospects. She does not expect much
from her lover in terms of friendship or sexual prowess. His power is
enough to attract her. She becomes an actress, playing whatever role is
required by the man. She will probably remain very lonely while the
lover is infatuated by her. To him she will seem so independent,
straightforward, understanding, sexy, discreet and different from his
wife that he cannot resist the temptation. He will feel flattered, and all
caution or consideration for his family flies out of the window.

The modern courtesan is simply not satisfied with her life as it is
and takes whatever measures she believes are necessary to change
things. Perhaps she is a casualty of life and love or sometimes a victim
of the men who take advantage of her weakness. She goes from lover
to lover, and she might hit the big time, catching a man in the public
eye. After a kiss-and-tell affair, she is usually left to fend for herself,

with perhaps the sole consolation of a hefty monetary reward. Contrary to her aspirations, she is in fact heading nowhere, and most people, including her friends and family, regard her as foolish. She is unlikely to experience real happiness as she will find it hard to return to a settled, ordinary life. Her lover returns to his family, sometimes stripped of his official duties, saying that he loves his wife and children and that he belongs with them. The mistress disappears, never to be heard of again. She has had her moment of glory, but she has lost the game and not achieved what she set out to accomplish. She has become redundant.

The only advice to the modern courtesan, or anybody contemplating becoming one, is that it is a strategy likely to cause great unhappiness and rarely brings about the gains in status or money anticipated, at least in the long term. She would be better off if she learnt to love herself and others, as she really is and they really are. The average woman will not make a fortune from her job. However, at least she will have self-respect, and the chances of meeting a man who will truly care for her will be vastly improved. It can make all the difference.

The single-minded mistress has different motives, and in contrast to her modern courtesan counterpart, can be married or single. If single, then she is with the lover for what he is, not because he's married. She is not looking to take advantage of his status, professionally or financially. She does not usually want to marry him. All in all, it is an arrangement which suits both parties.

She doesn't favour married men over single men, she just doesn't eliminate them as potential lovers. She may have been married before or had a few relationships, but none have been quite right. She is usually over thirty, mature, independent, fairly intelligent and unwilling to settle for second best. She has come to look upon her single status as something to be treasured and savoured. She is her own master: she decides what she wants from life, how she uses her money and what she does with her time. She makes no compromises.

Her life is satisfactory and she will only change it for the right man. She is a woman who knows what she can achieve in life and goes for it with abandon. Solitude is fine at times but she wants her share of male companionship, love and sex like anybody else. The proportion of single women has risen by a half since 1979, and 39 per cent of unmarried females are celibate.[4] One night stands are ill-advised because of the dangers of sexually transmitted diseases and besides, casual sex can be very unsatisfactory, especially for a woman. One mistress commented that she had stayed in her relationship because the lover provided a constant in her life. Sex, though lower down on

her list of needs than love and companionship, was an integral element
of her sense of well-being. Most women feel this to be true.

Good men are difficult to find and single men beyond their thirties
don't necessarily make the best lovers. They are often threatened by
problems like premature ejaculation and they can feel inadequate in
comparison with their married counterparts because they do not have
a long-term partner. They are either desperate for a lover, or fear
commitment. In the absence of the ideal (a single man), the married
man can therefore prove to be a great choice. Most are house-trained,
sexually more relaxed, willing to teach and occasionally be taught, and
of course they are guaranteed to be faithful in their fashion. Two
women are more than enough for most men.

The single-minded mistress has learnt to maintain the balance of
this relationship by her own rules. The sitting-around and waiting for
him to call is not for her, so she is likely to have arranged a set time
when they call each other regularly. He will let her know in advance
the dates he can see her, and they compare diaries and settle on the
ones that suit their schedules. In many ways these two are like a
married couple but with a difference. They understand each other's
motives and needs and they both exist at the fringes of each other's
lives. They exist in another dimension when they are together, a life
devoid of the mundane, a life where only they matter. The relationship
is often symbiotic, in the sense that each receives from the other what
they lack in their 'other life'. They support each other in bad times and
can become great friends.

The mistress has organized her life into compartments, not unlike
many male lovers. Emotionally detached from him, she can enjoy
others parts of her life when they are not together and does not miss
him to distraction, like many of her reluctant counterparts. She keeps
her options open, and probably goes out with other men, although she
doesn't necessarily have other sexual liaisons. It is this type of relationship that sometimes (though rarely nowadays) develops into a
long-term arrangement in which the lover supports the mistress financially. He might buy her a flat or give her an allowance; in effect she
becomes his second wife. Of course this changes the dynamics of the
relationship, as the mistress becomes financially dependent on the
lover.

Both the lover and the mistress might remain relatively happy with
the status quo for a considerable time. Life never stands still, however,
and eventually something will disturb the delicate balance. She may
have been a reluctant mistress who has accepted, wholly or partly, that
the lover will stay in his marriage. She loves him and does not want to

leave him, but realizes that the only way she can stay sane and keep him is to become a wanton mistress. This transition is not easy as she has to relegate her lover into a peripheral area of her life, similar to the way many lovers deal with their mistresses. As his position changes, the forces that maintain the triangle between lover, mistress and wife are disturbed.

The lover's relationship with his wife is usually distant. They are not very close and rarely share their feelings and experiences. Emotional energy is channelled towards the third party, the mistress, and this relationship is emotionally intense. The affair may therefore stabilize the marriage by keeping the real issues safely hidden. When the reluctant mistress becomes a wanton mistress her relationship with the lover becomes more distant. The lover's comfortable position is dislodged, and he may be forced to take a serious look at his marriage and his life.

The mistress will find that this emotional detachment allows her to assess life more objectively. Less embroiled in the affair and no longer spending most of her time thinking about him, she finds her attitudes and behaviour begin to change. She will see the relationship for what it is and often takes practical steps to alter her circumstances. She might start a new career or perhaps become more socially active. She will also be more open to new relationships. Sometimes this transformation results in a curious role reversal whereby the lover misses his emotional feed so much that he assumes the part of the reluctant mistress. Where as previously she would wait for the phone to ring and told her lover how much she missed him, now he calls her more frequently and tells her how he loves her and wants to be with her.

For the new-born wanton mistress, this is the beginning of the end. In many ways it is easier leaving the lover in this situation than when she was a reluctant mistress. Sometimes the relationship continues in the new format for quite some time, but as the balance has been disturbed, it is usually temporary. The mistress will find somebody else. It will happen because she will give out the signs that she is available for a new relationship, even if subconsciously. She may have previously let people assume that she has a boyfriend, thereby blocking her own chances, whereas now she will tell people that she has a part-time lover and is looking, or simply, that she has not got a boyfriend. The lover may leave her and rediscover his marriage, or decide to leave his wife as the new arrangement does not give him the emotional support he needs to maintain the status quo. He might just find another mistress.

Whatever her previous status, the single-minded mistress is affected

by the forces of the triangle. While not providing the emotional intensity, she may be a calming and balancing influence on the lover's
marriage. As long as she is content to accept that the relationship is
going nowhere, this set-up might work well for her. The wanton
mistress should, however, make sure that her future needs are not
compromised. An ideal arrangement today may not be so in the future.
Therefore, she should take stock at regular intervals and see whether
she is still content with her life's direction. If not, it is time to make
changes. She must make sure that her options are kept as open as
possible, and maintain her independence, both mental and financial.
Lastly, it would not hurt to have an active social life to ensure that she
at least has the opportunity to meet a man who could be the one for
her.

The married wanton mistress is not unlike her lover, in that she
does not usually want to leave the marriage. She is resolutely married,
and finds that an affair with a man in a similar situation relieves her of
anxieties that she might experience with a single lover. He will not
pester her into divorce and remarriage and will be as careful and
discreet as she to avoid the danger of getting caught. As with any
affair, there must be something wrong with both of their marriages for
the affair to begin in the first place. However, on the whole, both
might love their spouses and their families, although the type of love
might be expressed more in terms of care and trust than need or sexual
satisfaction.

One typical scenario is where the woman has married young, had
children, and in all the hectic bustle of the early years of marriage
somehow put aside her own needs. She had done the housework,
looked after the children and her husband, entertained the family and
common friends for years, and so there has been no time to think
about herself. The man she married may be respectable, kind-hearted
and good, but there is something in him and in his behaviour that
makes her scream inside. She might dread going on holiday with him,
or the prospect of his retirement. She is happiest when he is away, and,
often, the sexual side of their marriage has all but withered away.

The most trivial things can annoy her, and these are not the causes
but symptoms of the state of her marriage. He may read in bed and
keep her awake, watch television constantly, be a bingo addict, but
whatever he is or does, he adores her and puts her on a pedestal. He
has looked after her for years, is a good father, and may well be really
happy with the marriage. She feels bound to him. How could she ever
leave him when he hasn't done anything wrong? She might also worry
about how he would take it should she leave. She cannot see that he

could ever cope, and she might have visions of him committing suicide. She just couldn't treat him that way.

Another problem she will often have is that her earning power may be low. Over the years she has become used to a certain standard of living, and as she has often stayed at home with the children while they grew up, her skills willl be outdated. In short, she is dissatisfied, unhappy but also afraid to alter her circumstances in any way. She will usually feel a moral obligation to accept her lot, to stay with her husband, children and extended family.

When she meets a married man whom she is attracted to and/or finds suitable, she is probably at the stage where her children are near or at adult age and she has reached a kind of mid-life crisis. She wonders whether she should stay in a relationship which for her is life-less, joyless and sexless, but at the same time she doesn't know what awaits her on the other side. She accepts the duty towards her children and the responsibility it carries, but she wonders, all the same, whether she should leave the marriage. She may have worked hard to make the marriage a success but she is not fulfilled.

The relationship functions within the triangle, the dependencies working in harmony with both marriages. As long as this remains stable, the relationship cannot develop and is usually suffocated in time. The mistress has chosen to explore her options and this can be good for her. She keeps herself emotionally detached from the lover. She learns about herself as an individual, separate from her identity within the family, and this will either make her stronger in her marriage or give her the strength to leave it. She will experience the pain of guilt and betrayal, but she feels morally entitled to choose to do what she needs rather than what people around her expect and demand of her.

The problems that she might encounter fall into two groups. She might become emotionally attached and fall in love, or the dynamics of the affair might change. In the first case, she will become a reluc-tant mistress or, if her feelings are reciprocated, leave her marriage for the new relationship. In the latter case, either of the respective spouses might find out and expose the affair, or have affairs themselves, both of which will again change the dynamics of the foursome.

The single-minded, married, wanton mistress is compelled to engage in an affair either through plain boredom or a real need to find out what is missing in her life and marriage. The bored wife may be in an open marriage, where affairs are part of the arrangement, while the trapped wife may be afraid to step outside her familiar environment. Both run the risk of destroying what they have, but it is a conscious decision and perhaps a necessary step.

Sooner or later, she will have to decide what she wants from her life and marriage. Living between relationships is hard at the best of times because of the stress created by the need to conceal. She should, like her single counterpart, take stock of her life at regular intervals to see whether she is still content with her parallel lives or whether it is time to take decisive action, one way or the other. The choice will not become any easier with time – and it is wholly hers.

Any type of wanton mistress might want to possess the unattainable, experience the thrill of infatuation time after time, be an addict who loses interest as soon as she reaches her goal. A single man would not give her the satisfaction of capturing somebody else's husband in her web, having the excitement of something which is not hers. She might become a serial mistress who is unable to trust any man, single or married, as she has heard the lies and excuses all too often. She may also be an eternal bachelor, who fears commitment, and if her lover starts talking about divorce she will flee immediately.

Recent research into neurological personality disorders[5] claims that there are six categories of behaviour which exist in shadow form and which are flaws within a person's mental make-up. The theory is intriguing as it identifies these behaviours as originating in the structure and chemistry of the brain, albeit affected by the environment. The two behavioural groups that are of interest in this context are hypomania and attention deficit disorder. Hypomania is characterized by the charismatic professional whose thrill-seeking sexual behaviour threatens her downfall. Attention deficit disorder most commonly applies to the energetic, impatient executive who leaves a trail of unfinished sentences, projects and even marriages in her wake. Both types could be a blueprint for the serial wanton mistress. The researchers say that it may be a great help if the sufferer knows and understands the origin of her condition. She may then also be able to change direction if she so desires.

The wanton mistress conducts the relationship on her terms, and while it may be far from ideal, at least she is more or less in control of her destiny. Most of these women are happy to stay as they are, whether single or married. The reluctant mistress has a lot to learn from her in terms of managing the affair, and it may be advisable for her to consider changing her status from reluctant to wanton if she decides to stay in the relationship long term.

As long as the wanton mistress keeps questioning her motives regularly and making sure this is what she wants and what is best for her, the arrangement can work well. If she meets her ideal man, she can change the status quo, if not, she can continue the relationship with the married man. He, in time, will probably become a great friend and a source of happiness. As we know, divorce rates are soaring and many people stay in locked unhappy marriages. Perhaps the wanton mistress's way of life is preferable to marrying for the sake of it, or remaining in an unhappy marriage that does not work. Perhaps she has grabbed happiness or relief where she has found it. She might see this as her only chance to be happy with herself and her life, even if this conflicts with the rules of our society.

Relationships are the most difficult and important part of our lives to get right. Some of us marry successfully, some don't. If we divorce or have remained single, this does not necessarily mean that we are somehow lacking, or that we should give up love and sex for good.

5   The Lover

This is the man who occupies most of your thoughts and some of your dreams, yet he remains an elusive enigma that you will never truly understand. Although this is undoubtedly a significant contributor to his attraction, it causes untold problems. Statements beginning 'I just don't understand why . . .' typified our conversations with the mistresses we interviewed. This chapter aims to give you an insight into your lover's motives and feelings, his reasons for initiating the relationship in the first place and the way in which he views his mistress, his wife and himself.

There is no universal template for the typical adulterer. All men, be they vicar or villain, are potential candidates for infidelity. If the temptation is great enough and the opportunity is there, any man could find himself involved with someone other than his wife. There are no exceptions. However, many men do remain faithful, and although exact percentages are difficult to obtain, surveys estimate that between 25 and 50 per cent of husbands do not have any sexual partners other than their wives throughout their marriages. Infidelity, therefore, is quite common but bona fide mistresses are not. Therefore there must be something about the man who takes a mistress that sets him apart from other men. This is an aspect we plan to explore.

Lovers are often portrayed as the helpless victims of their mistresses' wiles and sometimes as insensitive womanizers. These assessments may indeed be relevant to men who indulge in casual affairs but for those who embark on deeper extramarital relationships the truth has little to do with either. They are neither as weak nor as uncaring as the two observations suggest.

Lovers are seldom questioned in depth about the reasons for their infidelities. It is assumed, often wrongly, that any man, given half a chance, would jump at the chance to bed another woman he found attractive provided, of course, he thought he could get away with it.

The fear of detection is the biggest deterrent to the married man since most are not seeking a way to destroy their marriages but are merely looking for a temporary diversion.

Whatever the characteristics of the lover, something about him manages to persuade his mistress that he is worth all the disadvantages that accompany the relationship. Each obviously has something to offer her that outweighs everything else, but trying to identify just what these elusive characteristics might be proved harder than we had supposed. He seems to be a man who enjoys the company of women, often appearing supremely confident, and one who has the opportunity to maintain an affair with little risk of detection. It is these last two aspects that mark the significant difference between him and those men who remain faithful: confidence and opportunity. Most lovers have to be able to hide their affairs from their wives, which means that they must have both the opportunity to meet their mistresses as a normal part of their day-to-day activities and the confidence to believe they can escape detection.

If we take a completely dispassionate view of these men, we can make some extremely uncomfortable observations. Most keep their affairs secret by deception. They will either lie openly to their wives, family and friends or deceive by sins of omission. Outwardly, and to all intents and purposes, they maintain the image of the husband and happy family man – an easy role to play in today's society – while leading the hidden life of a lover. This hypocrisy is often compounded by many lovers' double standards, in that they would not tolerate infidelity from either their wives or their mistresses. They also hurt, or run the risk of hurting, those they claim to care about because they put their own needs before all else. They seldom acknowledge their mistresses publicly and often have considerable difficulty choosing which woman they would rather be with. Their wives invariably win not necessarily because their husbands love them more but simply because they lack the courage to leave. And, finally, they are frighteningly naïve. They never expect to be found out.

These common traits are self-evident, but are seldom spelt out in the mistress's mind and, interestingly, most were suggested to us by the faithful men we interviewed. We found that, contrary to our belief, most men have little respect for those who are unfaithful, their condemnation being far more pointed than that of the women. It is possible that some of this condemnation could be the result of sour grapes and envy, but generally lovers are viewed as lacking in character and, at the very least, unfair by other members of their sex. However, despite the fact that the lover appears to be a rat, albeit a loveable rat, the mistress simply overlooks these flaws or else relegates them to the fourth division. It does not make sense, but that is what happens.

If the mistress's dilemma is that her heart rules her head, the lover's dilemma is just the opposite. Throughout the relationship, what and how he thinks determines how he manages both his marriage and his affair and persuades him, almost without exception, that staying with his wife is the best course of action. This is true even if he loves his mistress more than his wife. The emotional aspects of a relationship are simply not at the top of his list. It is, perhaps, this single fact that causes so much confusion for the mistress. The reason he stays, upsetting though it may be for her, is simple: that is what he wants most. The risk of condemnation and of losing the respect of his family and friends, the risk of losing his children, the overwhelming costs involved in divorce – all outweigh the love he might feel for another woman. She might win the fight against his wife, but it is so much more difficult to fight the social structures that work to enforce and protect the state of matrimony.

A recent report[1] that surveyed both men and women who had started affairs asked the question, 'What was the primary concern that you had when initiating the relationship?' Top of the list for women was that their feelings had overridden everything else, but married men put, as their chief concern, 'With care, this will not damage my marriage.' From the outset, they had decided that their marriages needed to be preserved. This immovable boundary around the marriage is what causes the lover to take a mistress rather than leave his wife for another woman in the first place. Despite this, the inviolate marriage does not stop him initiating an affair in the first place – which would seem the most logical thing to do.

We did talk to some men who had never been unfaithful. All spoke of the wish to preserve their marriages, and ultimately they believed that an affair was not worth the risk. The lover obviously does think it is worth it, which means he believes the risk to be minimal or non-existent. On the other hand, he might even enjoy the excitement of the risk or knows that his wife would not leave him if she found out.

Some years ago, when the adult population of Britain was canvassed on the question of happiness, it was discovered that the most contented people were married men, followed not by married women but by single women. This certainly challenges the cynical view that 'All women should be married – but no men.' Other significant revelations are that over 70 per cent of divorces in Great Britain are awarded to wives and that very few men abandon relationships without another woman to go to. This is not usually the case for women. To a certain extent, it could be said that men have more opportunities to find another partner since it is more socially acceptable for them to date younger women, thereby offering a larger pool of replacements to choose from. However, despite this, after divorce or separation, over 50 per cent of men say they regret the decision as opposed to only 30 per of women.

Men and women are different in their thinking processes, they are raised differently and they might even have brains that work differently. Psychologists debate at length the 'nurture versus nature' question to try to assess why people behave in certain ways, and while no definitive conclusions have emerged as yet there are numerous hypotheses. The fundamental issue is whether our behaviour, feelings and thought processes are affected more by our environment or more by fixed physiological and genetic patterns in our make-up. It is known, for example, that testosterone causes aggression and that men have significantly more of this hormone than women. This, then, marks a difference in behaviour which has a physical cause.

One theory suggests that men and women may have different brain structures. Women may have significantly more connections between the left and right hemispheres of their brains than men. When a woman communicates, she uses many areas of her brain simultaneously, whereas a man uses only a few. This potentially increases the information available to women at any point in time and affects the ways in which they manage and process it. To what extent this might affect the way the sexes feel and think is still debatable, but it would help to explain both women's intuition and their ability to handle many things at the same time as well as men's single-mindedness and apparent lack of emotion.

As far as our upbringing is concerned, parents still treat their male and female children differently. Society treats men and women differently. Despite greater sexual equality, and despite growing awareness of our double standards, there are still different expectations of how boys and girls, men and women, are supposed to behave. In particular, men are expected to show less emotion than women, yet they have written among the best love songs we have ever heard. The emotion is there, it is just expressed differently and is acted upon less.

This book cannot address this subject of men and women's differences in detail but we have introduced these notions to illustrate the confusion that prevails. It is hardly surprising, therefore, that men and women often have great difficulty understanding each other, especially in affairs of the heart, where emotion plays such a strong role for both.

The research for this chapter was a voyage into the unknown for us, since we were no wiser than the next woman when it came to understanding our lovers' motivations. We made two very significant discoveries. The first was the willingness of men to talk to us about their situations. We had supposed they might be reluctant to talk about what we felt was a sensitive subject. However, they welcomed the opportunity, some even saying that it was a great relief to be able to speak openly about their relationships, often for the first time. We found that, unlike women, men do not have the same kinds of support structures for sharing emotions, and many had not been able to discuss their feelings and thoughts with anyone.

The second discovery was that the lover's attitude to his mistress and her place within his life was considerably different to what we had supposed it to be. Without exception, the men described a deep and significant relationship, wholly different to the marriage but nevertheless of great importance. Yet none really considered the other woman to be a mistress as such. She was most often referred to as 'my girlfriend'. When questioned, these men described a mistress as a kept woman; the very fact that few felt or were responsible for the maintenance of their 'girlfriends' automatically meant that they could not therefore be mistresses.

All men differentiate between flings and a more permanent relationship with a mistress – the former has little emotional significance for them whereas the latter does. No matter whether the man was by nature faithful, a partner of an open marriage or an outright philanderer, his mistress represented a powerful influence in his life – an influence he felt compelled to control in the best way he could in order, ultimately, to preserve his marriage.

Most affairs start in the workplace, most happen by chance and most are short-lived. The vast majority are based, mostly for the men and often for the women, on an initial powerful sexual attraction. Few of the lovers we interviewed were seeking a mistress, but rather a short-term, no-strings-attached fling. Those men admitting to wanting a relationship of more depth had all had mistresses before and were keen to repeat the experience. None said that they were looking for a way out of their marriage, but all recognized that there were deficiencies in their relationships with their wives. Those men who are looking for escape (rather than escapism) are much more likely to leave their wives than take up mistresses.

The type of woman the man might approach is often very different from his wife in terms of her personality, looks, status and age. If his wife is quiet, his mistress is likely to be an extrovert. If his wife is unemotional, his mistress may be more comfortable expressing her feelings. If his wife is beautiful, his mistress may be plain. If his wife is a career woman, his mistress may be domestic. He is looking for something he cannot find within his marriage. It is generally believed that most mistresses are considerably younger than their lovers' wives. Although this tends to be common with casual affairs, or in those situations where a man pays for his mistress, or when he actually leaves his wife, this does not appear to be the case in long-term mistress/lover relationships. The age differential, where it exists, is usually there because of the initial physical attraction between the two parties.

It is a sad but undeniable fact that men are more concerned than women with the physical attributes of their partners, and younger women do tend to be more attractive to most men. An older woman might, moreover, know better than to initiate a relationship with a married man, but this cannot be relied upon since a number of the women we interviewed were in their forties and fifties, and some, although very few, were actually older than their lovers' wives. Furthermore a younger woman is unlikely to remain content in a relationship where she has so little to gain and, if we are honest, has more potential replacements to choose from.

We have already explored in some detail the reasons for initiating extramarital affairs. These can be summarized as boredom, revenge, escapism, simple serendipity or the lack of sex or companionship; the last reason is the most common. The majority of male lovers interviewed wanted and expected only a temporary, simple and pleasurable liaison, which they intended to leave as soon as it became too complicated. Therefore, when the relationship deepens, we can safely say that something has gone horribly wrong for him. He suddenly finds that he has fallen in love with another woman, something he truly never meant to happen. Given his realization that he now has two women in his life, neither of whom he wants to give up and each of whom he cares for, albeit in different ways, he needs to consider what to do next. If he still persists with the precept that his marriage must be preserved, for whatever reasons, he manages this situation in the only way he can. If the woman is willing, he will maintain the new relationship alongside his marriage.

Many lovers appear to be emotionally constrained in some way. Both parties to the affair remark on this but from different perspectives. Lovers talk of a freedom of expression and behaviour within their relationships with their mistresses that does not appear to exist within their marriages. Mistresses remark upon the way in which their lovers appear to be able to compartmentalize their lives and wonder at the way they can control the passion they so obviously feel. Rather than lacking feelings, as the mistress might observe, it is possible that the lover is in fact an extremely emotional person, perhaps more so than the average man. His upbringing, his life and his marriage deny him the opportunity to express and fulfil the feelings he has and therefore he might feel compelled to find an outlet. Many men who take mistresses do so in their later years, at a time when most people are more relaxed about the way they feel. The so-called 'male menopause' has been cited as a hypothetical reason for a man suddenly taking a mistress, but maybe he simply feels he no longer has to conform.

There are essentially three situations – two distinct and one hybrid – in which a man might find himself with a mistress. The first, and the one we have concentrated on so far, characterizes the situation in which he has fallen in love with a woman other than his wife and wants to maintain both relationships. The mistress loves him and this decision, for both, is predominately based on emotion. The second comprises those situations, often featured in the popular press, in which the man will approach (or be approached by) a woman who is willing to be his mistress in exchange for her upkeep or some other external gain. This is essentially a business arrangement, in which love seldom plays a part and the decision is predominately rational. The third defines the transition from situation one to situation two, in which the lover will offer a woman with whom he has fallen in love (and who loves him) a business arrangement in order to ensure that she will not leave him.

We do not propose to explore business arrangements in great detail in this chapter. They are the most publicized and clearest to understand since they involve little or no emotional complications. However, the mistresses in these relationships are the ones most likely to kiss and tell. Despite the fact that the lover may feel more secure because a deal of some kind has been struck, he is in fact more vulnerable. This is because the mistress, if she is not in love, does not have the same kind of concern and affection for him. Men, it appears, are not good judges of women, especially wanton mistresses. We have all been astounded by the newspaper revelations that indicate the extent to which some lovers expose themselves to danger. He trusts the mistress because they have an arrangement, whereas he should trust her only when she truly loves him – and maybe not even then.

The boundaries and terms and conditions of the business arrangement are usually established at the outset. The man involved generally feels no need to justify his position and his potential mistress tends to be aware of the ground rules. She, like him, makes a rational decision about the relationship. However, for those relationships that are not so clearly defined, male lovers tend to explain why, when they are married, they are trying to woo another woman. They think that they need to justify their actions to her and to protect the position of the marriage from the outset.

From the lover's perspective, the progression from fling to relationship offers some insights into the fundamental differences between a man and a woman in love. We are going to attempt to translate what men have told us into comments to which, we trust, women can relate. We asked mistresses for some of the most common statements made by their lovers in the early days of their relationships. We then reviewed these with the men we interviewed in an attempt to find an honest translation, thereby uncovering their true meanings.

'I love my wife, I will never leave her'

He might or might not admit love for his wife at this stage, but will generally make clear his determination to maintain his marriage. He believes he is setting expectations from the outset and thereby hopes to short-circuit any possible demands that might involve him having to leave home. He is quite simply stating his escape clause and showing that his approach is not serious. With this, he assures himself that he is being honest and can safely store the phrase 'But I told you at the beginning . . .' for future use. It is also probable that, at the same time, he is testing the ground to see what he can get away with. If the woman walks away, little is lost; if she does not, he assumes that she accepts the provisional nature of his proposition. He does not consider for one moment that the woman might not believe him or, indeed, hardly listen to him at all. At the beginning, she is rarely considering the break-up of his marriage – this only becomes an issue later in the relationship.

The woman perceives that, by approaching her, he is not only risking hurting his wife, whom he claims to love, but also risking the marriage that he claims to want to maintain. For most women, this is a paradox; for most men it is quite simple. He is taking a calculated risk and believes he can get away with it without losing his wife. If he does indeed love his wife, this will also confirm the suspicion that most men have little difficulty separating love from sex. Most women find this extremely difficult to do and are more likely than men to become emotionally involved after sex. In this the lover has an initial advantage over the mistress. He sees no contradiction in loving his wife and sleeping with someone else. In short, he means what he is saying and the woman should believe him.

'We have an open marriage – she sleeps with whomever she wants to and so do I'
While single mistresses are normally monogamous the partners in an open marriage, by definition, are not. This man is not faithful to his wife – by mutual agreement – and vice versa. He is telling his potential mistress that his marriage has survived situations like this before and that she will be another liaison that he will, in all probability, tell his wife about. Members of an open marriage sustain their relationship by using third parties to alleviate shortcomings in the marriage mostly founded on sexual or intellectual boredom. Most studies into open marriage consider the effect of such arrangements only on the marriage itself and conveniently ignore the effect of extramarital affairs on the third parties involved. Generally speaking, this is an extremely precarious situation for the mistress, since the lover's wife is complicit in the relationship and will know about it from the outset. Such marriages exploit third parties by design and should therefore only be entered into by those with extremely robust emotions.

'My wife doesn't understand me' etc.
Under this collective heading goes the list of all the things that could be missing from his marriage and/or the poor way in which he is treated. Elements of this category of statements will occur throughout the relationship and are in all probability reasonably true. The lover is looking for sympathy and understanding and appeals to the woman's mothering instinct. This is not necessarily done on purpose, but can be extremely effective nonetheless. Despite his tales of woe he is not driven to abandon his marriage and the mistress might consider asking him why, given his complaints, he stays.

Although it does not follow that his mistress will understand him any better than his wife, most of the long-standing male lovers we interviewed believed this to be the case. They also tended to discuss issues with their mistresses that they did not discuss with their wives and gave us three main reasons for this. First, some men felt the need to protect their wives from many of their personal problems and concerns since they felt that they had to be the one who was strong and in control. Secondly, others feared derision from their wives if they showed weakness and, lastly they thought that their wives might not be interested or able to help anyway. Most wives do not share or understand their husbands' business interests. Most mistresses are single and usually self-supporting professional women. It therefore follows that they are better able to appreciate the pressures the male lover faces at work and the effect this has on both his private and professional life. In addition, mistresses tend to be more tolerant – they feel they have to be.

Men regard the marriage, wife and family as their responsibility, almost like a job they have to do and do well. They do not view their mistresses in the same way and when this sense of duty is removed, they feel more able to discuss their vulnerabilities.

The mistress must constantly remind herself that, at least at the beginning of the relationship, her lover's wife understands him much better than she does. Reluctant as the mistress may be to see his wife in a positive light, she would be prudent to consider the other side of the stories he tells. It really cannot be that bad or he would not still be there.

'My wife is having an affair'

He is probably inviting the woman to be part of his revenge attack and hopes to restore his self-esteem in the process. By presenting himself in a vulnerable light, it is also an extreme example of the 'my wife doesn't understand me' category. However, if revenge is his primary motive, this is highly dangerous as he obviously intends to get even for selfish reasons and use the potential mistress in the process. If he is trying to restore his damaged ego (men do not cope well with the sexual infidelities of their partners), it is important to understand whether he wants to maintain the marriage or whether he is looking to establish a safety net to catch him if his wife leaves. Only the last case offers any kind of hope for the woman he is approaching and, even then, it would be far better if he did the leaving rather than his wife.

'I like my wife, but I stopped loving her years ago'

This should give a clue about the potential lover's priorities in his marriage. Love isn't high on the list or he would have left her – years ago. He wants a mistress to supply him with the love and affection that he is intimating he needs but which is missing from his marriage. Thereby she would enable him to stay within a loveless union with his wife. He is obviously bound to his wife by many other factors. These could be friendship, children, feelings of gratitude, a sense of duty or responsibility, habit, financial considerations, his career and even a fear of admitting failure. The chances are that these bonds have evolved over a long time and will probably continue to outweigh any advantages offered by his mistress.

'I would have left years ago if it wasn't for the children; perhaps when they're older . . .'

For most people, children are a reason for choosing to stay married, even unhappily. They are a valid and commendable reason for maintaining a marriage provided the environment is not detrimental to the children's well-being. The man who cites his children as a reason for staying married at the beginning of the relationship will continue to use this throughout. Children might grow up but they never disappear – ask your parents!

'I am separated/getting separated/waiting for a divorce'
Some men do not admit they are married at the beginning of an affair, although this is becoming less common as social attitudes to infidelity soften. Others might tell the mistress that they hope to be free in the medium term, thereby dangling the carrot of a normal relationship in the near future. We did not interview any men who admitted lying about their marital status, but we understand that the promise of a separation or a divorce is sometimes used to entice women who might otherwise decline the offer of a relationship.

Anyone on the verge of a marriage break-up is vulnerable and distressed. This is true even if they know that the relationship was wrong and must end. To initiate an affair when someone is in this frame of mind is always fraught with difficulties, and it is best, if possible, to encourage them to spend time alone before embarking on a new romance. But at the very least, it is best to believe nothing until the divorce is absolute.

'I'm different from other married men'
This statement is a prime example of the male ego, by which he is trying to set himself apart from the bad press that philanderers receive. He never seems to expand on exactly how he is different and, amazingly, no one ever asks him. One is left to draw one's own conclusions. It is therefore imperative that he be asked for details; significantly, although we asked our male interviewees to elaborate, we could not get a straight answer from any of them. We suppose he might be right of course – everyone is entitled to the benefit of the doubt. However, when it comes to their infidelities, their motivations and the way in which they handle their extramarital affairs, most such men fit squarely into the familiar pattern.

'My wife and I do not sleep together any more'
It really is surprising how many immaculate conceptions there are . . .

Whatever the lover says, it all seems to make perfect sense at the time and generally does little to deter the mistress. Essentially, he is speaking to her head and her head is hardly listening at all.

It is instructive to chart the development of the relationship from fling to affair from the man's perspective. At the beginning, all speak of the adrenalin rush occasioned by the forbidden nature of the liaisons and the stimulation of sex with a new woman. However, as anyone will testify, this level of excitement cannot be maintained forever and slowly the relationship changes. The waning of this excitement should in theory signal the time for the man to leave and return home to the safety of his marriage. Indeed, this is what most men do.

However, for a few the relationship does not remain a superficial one based on sex and excitement alone. The lover finds that he likes his mistress, enjoys her company and is beginning to make significant comparisons between her and his wife. He wonders what it would be like if he was with his mistress permanently. He thinks about her and endures endless battles between his heart and head which are never truly resolved. In many cases, his heart is with his mistress whereas his head is with his wife.

This phase, which occurs most commonly after six to twelve months, marks a significant turning-point for the lover. Up until this time he has been totally in control. His emotions are manageable and he is having a good time. When the issue of choice is raised, it is raised by the way he feels. Now he is not having such a good time – this was not supposed to happen. He finds that he does not want to lose his mistress. He knows by now, whether she has told him or not, that she is unhappy with the situation and wants more and he begins to fear losing her. If he is going to leave home, he will leave now, but, as all of us know, this is extremely unlikely. So he is left with a dilemma: how to keep his mistress while, at the same time, denying her what she wants most – a future with him.

The different approaches he might now take are directly dependent on the strength of his emotional control. He might decide to allow the relationship to cool off in an attempt to take stock and this is signalled to the mistress as him pulling away. Many mistresses have great difficulty coping with this kind of behaviour, since at some intuitive level they see the coldness but sense the underlying passion. Being the insecure people that they most often are, mistresses will try to convince themselves that what they sense is purely wishful thinking on their part and that they are about to lose the most important person in their lives. This is seldom true; it is merely that their lovers are withdrawing because they cannot cope with their feelings. This is common behaviour for most men (and even some women), and the best thing that a mistress can do in these situations is to be supportive but avoid the temptation to try to engage her lover in deep and meaningful conversations. He will not want to discuss his actions with anyone and is unlikely to talk about his feelings, even to his close friends. This phase is also dangerous from the point of view of his home life. His wife, too, is likely to recognize that all is not well, either because of his withdrawal or because he is overcompensating at home to try to disguise his inner turmoil.

When he believes his feelings are under control, he will return to the relationship. This will happen time and time again within the affair, since the lover will refuse to succumb to his feelings to the extent that they would cause him to leave home.

Another common approach is for the lover to introduce elements of his home life into his relationship with his mistress. He will want to tell her about his family, especially his children, the activities they share and the people they know and meet. This is done both to reinforce the fact that he is married and, more importantly, to remind him of his marriage at a time when he might be prone to forget. By doing this he uses his family as a mental talisman to protect him from the emotional temptation of his mistress.

He will take his marriage into his affair, but he will not take his affair into his marriage. Even if his wife knows about his affair, he is unlikely to discuss his mistress with her. The fact that he does tell his mistress so much illustrates two important points. The first is that he does not set the same boundaries for the affair as for the marriage and the second is that he is freer to discuss his life, at all levels, with his mistress. As painful as the mistress might find it to have to listen to details of his other life, the fact that he talks to her is meant as a great compliment and not the slight she sometimes feels it to be.

At home he will carry on quite normally, often feeling little or no guilt about his infidelity, because he has convinced himself that the marriage is safe, he is still continuing to provide for his family and is, by majority, fulfilling all his obligations. He has the ability, with careful management, to keep both lives distinct. However, the more he considers the possibility of leaving home, the guiltier he feels. As one man put it, 'It's like considering sacking someone who hasn't really done a bad job.'

He takes full responsibility for his wife and family. Seeing them as dependants, he sustains them and tries to protect them. If he were less caring about these people with whom he has shared so much, it is unlikely that his mistress would have the same level of respect for him. She is all too aware of the tremendous dilemma that he may be facing and fluctuates between her desire for him to leave home and her acceptance for his reasons for staying. It is this understanding, above all others, that causes her to try, to the best of her ability, to accept the role of mistress and that causes her to avoid forcing him into making a painful choice.

Men are more acutely aware than women of social structures and conventions. If they get divorced, it is viewed as a public failure, and they fear the condemnation from society at large and their extended family much more than from their wives. The pressures to be seen as successful pervade all that most men do and this includes their roles as husbands and fathers.

The lover often feels guilty about his mistress, although he will seldom tell her so. Every lover knows that the situation is not fair on her and, despite the fact that he keeps telling himself that she knows the score, he is affected quite strongly when she gets upset. However, he will seldom consider ending the relationship; he leaves this responsibility to her. He knows that he is unlikely to try to stop her if she does leave, since he is not prepared to offer the incentive she wants to make her stay. Most mistresses believe that if they make too many demands or become too emotional, their lovers will eventually walk away and return to the safety net of their marriages. The truth is that if he cares deeply about her, he will not walk away – he expects her to leave him instead and is often quite amazed when she does not.

If a lover is going to end the relationship, ignoring the obvious possibility that it might end because he stops loving his mistress, it will be when he can no longer sustain the two relationships and feels he has to make a choice. The reasons for this can range from the fact that his time is becoming more limited to the possibility that he can no longer cope with the emotional turmoil, or that either his wife or his mistress has issued an ultimatum. Once he has made his decision, little can be done to change his mind. The decision will be made by a brain which is extremely strong and very much in control of the situation. He will convince himself that 'a man's gotta do what a man's gotta do' and go.

Many men have affairs and a few take mistresses, but seldom do they leave their wives for their new loves. A friend asked how she could tell whether a potential lover was likely to be a member of this last small minority or not. All we can suggest is that she asks the man at the earliest opportunity, 'Have you ever considered that I might be a threat to your marriage?' If his answer is no, then she should realize that his marriage is a threat to her and walk away. If he is one of that courageous, small minority, he will follow her.

6   The Married Mistress

As a married mistress, you embody characteristics associated not only with the single mistress, but also those of the lover. This chapter supplements the preceding chapters since you will find that elements of all of them will also be relevant to you. You might suffer some or all of the pains of the single mistress and enjoy the same senses of elation and hope. Like the male lover, however, you have the additional responsibility of a spouse and possibly children. However, your situation is different to both in several ways. This chapter aims to highlight these differences and to explore the additional complexities of those affairs in which both parties are married – to somebody else.

Today, the true married mistress is extremely rare. In the past it was considered bad form to take a mistress who was not already married for two main reasons. First, an unmarried woman who had an affair ran the risk of ruining her reputation and would seldom be able to find a husband afterwards. Second, a married woman's financial support was guaranteed by her husband, not by her lover. Both points illustrate the fact that in the past very few women were able to sustain themselves independent of men. Now the situation is very different. Single women no longer have to rely upon men for their future security; they can provide for themselves. In as much as being a mistress would ever be sanctioned by society, it is now seen as more acceptable for a single woman to fulfil this role than one who is married.

Most unfaithful married women either have short-term affairs or flings lasting on average six months. Very few ever become mistresses. The main reason for this is the tremendous difficulty of sustaining and developing the relationship over a long period of time. In cases where the lover is also married both parties are restricted in terms of places they can meet. They have to hide their affair from their families and be able to account for time away from home. This, together with the woman's unwillingness to sustain a relationship that constantly threatens her home base, without the potential for a fruitful outcome, commonly causes her to force the affair to an early conclusion. She, much more than her single counterpart, is likely to ask her lover to leave his wife relatively early in the relationship, and if he does not, then she will probably leave him.

The risk of discovery is doubled and the parties involved both bear the emotional strain of deceit. This causes additional tensions in an already tense relationship. Men are better at compartmentalization. Women find this extremely difficult, especially in matters of the heart, and will find maintaining a double life very stressful. This increases the pressure on them to seek an early resolution.

The married woman, like her lover, risks her marriage throughout the affair, but, unlike the lover, this risk is a constant reality for her. Women tend to look and plan ahead and spend many hours agonizing over potential consequences. Men tend to live much more in the present and do not punish themselves with a constant barrage of 'what if' scenarios. The lover, therefore, does not concern himself unduly about the future of the affair. Women spend a great deal of time brooding about things that have not yet happened, and in particular the married mistress worries continually about discovery.

The married mistress is similar to the lover in that she too will have to deceive her family and possibly some or all of her friends. Most of her friends will know, and probably like, her husband. Some may not be happy to be made a party to her secret and she is therefore likely to have fewer support structures than a single mistress. Married men have a 'three wise monkeys' attitude to each other's infidelities. It is an accepted phenomenon. Women do not feel the same way, not even about each other, and other married women are more likely to view mistresses with suspicion and antagonism than with support and discretion.

One of the main problems the married mistress faces is that she is likely to be financially dependent upon her spouse. This is seldom true for the male lover. In many cases she does not earn enough to be able to sustain herself should the marriage end and she finds herself on her own. It is often this real, or perceived, dependence which causes her to stay within a marriage she believes she no longer wants. Financial dependence is, of course, not the only kind of dependence. She may have developed, like the lover, a dependence on being married itself, its general acceptability and the habit of day-to-day living. While not as exciting as an affair, it is certainly safer. Generally in the home she is cared for and, for the most part, she feels secure there.

The married mistress may also still love her husband. Perhaps it is a different love to the one she bears her lover, but it is a love that has grown and matured over many years. Many people would ascertain that if one loved one's spouse, one could not be unfaithful. However, this is an over-simplification. It is more likely to be the lack of communication and general closeness, that can happen over time in any marriage, that pushes people into affairs. There are also many different kinds of love. The more she cares about her husband, the guiltier she will feel, and it is often this guilt which will hasten the affair's demise.

As we saw in Chapter 5, the majority of men who initiate an adulterous relationship fully intend to preserve their marriages above all else. Married women do not have the same kind of dispassionate and calculated view when entering into the affair. Along with single women, they still maintain that it is strong emotion that propels them into their affairs and, unfortunately, preservation of the marriage comes a poor second. Most assert that the emotion had to be strong because it had to overcome the sense of duty and responsibility they felt towards their marriages.

When the affair begins, a married woman will presume that the lover views the consequences in the same way as she does and feels as she does. Both are married and she assumes that this commonality links their attitudes. She may therefore deduce that the man's approach is serious enough to constitute a threat to his marriage. Often nothing could be farther from the truth. As we have seen from the previous chapters, most such men do not regard their marriages as imperilled; consequences come later. They can also separate sex from love with little difficulty, whereas women find this much harder, if not impossible. Even if the emotional involvement is absent at the beginning, after the intimacy of a sexual relationship it will follow soon afterwards for most women.

An American film[1] features a telling quotation in which the hero, played by Walter Matthau, is instructed: 'Never have an affair with someone who has less to lose than you do.' In the film the logic behind this statement led to the conclusion that a married woman is far safer for a casual affair and less likely to create a fuss than a single woman. Many men share this perspective in real life. It is therefore highly probable that a married man who approaches a married woman believes that the potential affair will be far less involved, and therefore more fun, than one with a single woman. For flings he might even be correct; but for long-term relationships his presumption that a married woman would set the same priorities as him is highly misguided.

To illustrate this point, a woman we interviewed told us that at the beginning of the affair her lover said, 'It's good that you've got some-one else too – that will stop you getting too emotionally involved.' We cannot print her exact answer, but his statement indicates his reason-ing all too clearly. In fact for this particular mistress, having a partner made her decision to proceed with the affair more difficult, not easier, and this applies to most married women. For the man, the opposite was clearly true. Eventually, she left her partner rather than two-time him. Her lover did not leave his wife. This outcome is not unusual. We know of a number of married women who, having left their husbands, are still waiting for their lovers to leave home years later.

Women are more likely to follow their hearts than men; they are cited as being more emotional and less rational human beings. Reasoning and emotion are not mutually exclusive, however. A woman might rationally decide to follow her heart rather than her head. People are told that this is a bad thing to do, but we believe it is simply a different thing to do. If the world relied upon pure logic all the time, no room would be left for compassion, self-sacrifice, charity, hope, belief and, of course, love. True, emotion has its negative sides, but so too does reason.

Married women who leave their husbands to pursue a new love have also often left their children, despite the social condemnation. Motherly instincts are presumed to far outweigh fatherly instincts although we do not believe this is proven. However, most would casti-gate the woman far more for leaving her children than for leaving her husband, and she knows this.

Overall, married women's reasons for being unfaithful are not dissimilar to married men's, but few go looking for an affair. In most cases, the affair comes to them. They are also less likely to be unfaith-ful if they consider their marriages to be both happy and fulfilling. A man will often view his affair as a supplement, whereas a woman will eventually view it as a potential replacement for her marriage. She therefore will both look for and expect more than her lover.

If she is both sustained and protected within her marriage, this is the base from which she runs her life. She feels the need to protect this environment and is therefore less likely to be casually unfaithful than a man. The more dependent on this base she feels, the more she will resist temptation. The thought of trading something for nothing is not one she wants to entertain. However, if she believes that her lover does want a future with her, she would often be prepared to leave, thereby exchanging one base for another. The man who targets such a married woman may have to work considerably harder to win her than he might suppose. She might mistake his persistence as an indication of his seriousness, which, unfortunately, is not necessarily the case.

In order to become a bona fide mistress, a married woman has to establish a routine whereby she is free to meet her lover indefinitely. She might find a single friend who will lend her home, but usually meetings will be either on neutral ground (such as a hotel) or, occasionally, even in her own home. We have spoken to several married mistresses who used their homes for meetings. Interestingly no one ever met their lover in his home. There were three main reasons for this. The lover's wife was usually present, the mistress was unable to relax in the lover's home or the lover would not allow it. He might be content to meet in her home, but not in his. This is symbolic of the different perceptions of the affair. The man keeps his affair separate from his home life, while the woman joins them together.

For the married mistress, the longer the affair continues, the more she is likely to become dissatisfied with her life with her husband. The reverse is often the case for her lover. She may be fond of her husband, but many speak of feeling as if they are being unfaithful to their lovers rather than to their husbands during the course of the affair. She does not want to hurt her husband. She does not want to hurt her children. She does not want to hurt her parents and in-laws. She tries to convince herself that she is lucky to have a home and family and constantly berates herself for putting all this at risk. If her children are small, she worries about the effect of a divorce. If they are grown-up, she worries about their possible reaction. In short, she worries about everything.

If her marriage is intolerable, she would have already considered leaving. In most cases it is not intolerable, it is simply not enough for her. Most wives and mothers labour under the responsibility of service to their families, especially if the husband is the major breadwinner. This is one of the ways in which she pays for her keep. The role of wife and mother can make her self-sacrificing to the demands of her home and children, and many of the problems she faces are associated with the resultant loss of identity. Of course this is not true for every woman, nor for every mother, but nevertheless it is very common.

If such a woman becomes involves with another man, she will initially believe that she has no right to put herself, her feelings and requirements, first. However, if her lover can suddenly provide her with the identity she feels she has lost, her life changes dramatically. Suddenly she becomes a person in her own right, someone who is desirable again, one who is not taken for granted and whose opinions are sought and listened to. This can be a major factor in affecting the way she feels about her lover and is undoubtedly one of the key aspects of the relationship. She feels alive and an individual again.

Single mistresses have one major advantage over married mistresses in that they can build a life, albeit a part-time life, with their lovers in their own homes. This is a place where both can relax, an oasis that has the semblance of normality and affords them some peace and security. The lover can ring her whenever he wants to and she can call him without worrying about his telephone number appearing on her bill. He can write to her and send her presents with a freedom that the married woman yearns for. The single mistress also does not have the added responsibility of husband and children so, relatively speaking, her conscience is clearer than her married counterpart. The only real advantage that the married mistress has is the safety net of her marriage, which supports her now and is likely to continue to do so after the affair ends.

If the lover hopes to control the affair, limited access to his mistress is desirable and makes the affair more manageable; this often suits him well. It helps him to manage the rate at which the relationship can develop and gives him long gaps between meetings during which he can recover himself and return to the normality of his other life. This helps to distance himself and lessen his commitment to the relationship. On the other hand, if the affair does deepen, the pure frustration of the situation may force an early decision. It can work either way.

Another important fact to consider is that the single mistress can cry when she wants to. If times are bad, there is nothing to stop her releasing her emotion in the privacy of her own home. For the married mistress no such luxury exists. Whether things are going well or badly she must strive constantly to hide her feelings; this simply exacerbates the pressures under which she operates the affair. Few can bear the strain over a long period. If the affair continues, it means that her emotions have to be strong enough to overcome her isolation, her basic morality, her sense of loyalty and her fear. This makes the end of the affair even more critical for her. If she loses her lover, she also risks losing her self-respect having sacrificed her basic principles, perhaps for nothing. If the relationship does end, she cannot publicly mourn the loss of her lover, and the period after the end of the affair will be particularly hard to bear. She cannot show her grief, has few people she can talk to and nowhere to hide.

If the relationship between married lover and married mistress develops, despite all the barriers to be overcome, they can find themselves in similar circumstances. Although they may be in love with each other, they still cling to their marriages and for very similar reasons. The affair can reach an impasse where each is waiting for the other to take decisive action. Neither wants to burn their bridges and both seem to believe that the marriage is better than nothing. At this stage, there will either be a confrontation or a tacit agreement to continue with the affair while maintaining both marriages. The former is the most likely action for the woman, the latter the preferred outcome for the man. In all the situations we have encountered in which two people leave their marriages to be together, the break was invariably initiated by the woman.

If the affair continues it has little chance of development for either party. Slim though the possibility of a future may still be, at least a single mistress is free to find opportunities for the relationship's growth. When both are married, and neither will leave their marriages, such scope is severely limited.

If one of the parties wants more than the current situation offers, the dissatisfaction will grow and the risk will begin to look much less worthwhile. If neither wants more, the relationship has nowhere to go and will eventually start to fade. The freedom to explore new possibilities is so negligible that eventually one or other of the parties will walk away – usually the one whose aspirations have not been realized.

The fear of discovery is ever present, and the married mistress often wonders what her husband's reaction would be if he found out about her infidelity. The more emotionally involved she becomes with her lover, the harder it becomes for her to hide her feelings. Her husband might eventually notice changes in her mood, behaviour and appearance and become suspicious. On the other hand, unable to cope with the situation any longer, she might tell him, or perhaps someone else will. If he does find out, his initial reaction is likely to be shock. Everyone is always more surprised at female infidelity than male infidelity.

He may feel as if his territory has been invaded and will certainly wonder about how he measures up in the bedroom. His pride might also make him fear derision from other men – the cuckold is always seen as an object of pity and scorn. It was reported that Peter Parker Bowles knew about his wife's relationship with Prince Charles for many years. Yet it was only after Prince Charles finally admitted this fact on television, thereby confirming the rumours, that he asked for a divorce from Camilla. Before this it appeared that he could, and did, live with it.

The married mistress's husband will also realize that the affair was unlikely to have been undertaken for the sake of casual sex and was therefore meaningful to his wife. As a result he will suffer pain, humiliation and self-doubt. Men tend to be less forgiving than women, and whether he leaves her or not, he will never forget what has happened. Things will never quite be the same again.

A very few husbands, and we stress very few, might actually welcome the infidelity. It could be that they are playing around too and this will help to assuage their guilt. It could be that they see this as a perfect opportunity to initiate an affair themselves. It could be that they no longer care about sex and welcome the fact that the lover can fulfil that part of the marriage. It could be that they are actually titillated by the vision of someone else bedding their wives. So if his reaction is not one of shock and horror, he may have some interesting ulterior motives.

If the marriage continues, most parents decide not to tell small children about the affair. Having said this, children are particularly sensitive to bad feelings between their mothers and fathers and often react to unhappiness in the home. If the children are older, they might already have guessed or even be a party to the infidelity. In a very few cases, where parent and child are particularly close, the child may have been told about the affair while it is happening. This happens with women more than men. In nearly all cases, the child will not be supportive of the third party, even if they continue to support the parent who had the affair.

If children find out about the affair only after its discovery, their reactions will vary considerably depending upon their age, whether they still live at home or not and their current relationships with both parents. This is covered in detail in Chapter 7, but, in summary, the younger they are, the more frightened they will be and the older they are, the more angry they will be. Either way, they will be affected by this apparent schism in their parents' marriage and will need reassurance. It is not uncommon for children to take sides, willingly or unwillingly. They are more likely to support the injured party, and their animosity and condemnation is often considerably more difficult to address than the turmoil between husband and wife.

Most children, being self-centred, will be inclined to take the affair as a personal betrayal and threat. They will tend to be more concerned about the effect it might have on their lives than on that of their parents. Because of their vulnerability, all efforts must be made to protect young and teenage children from the affair and its aftermath. If this proves impossible, considerable time must be invested in reassurance. For older children, there can be no rules. The extent to which they can be included is directly linked to the way in which they relate to their parents. However, once the affair is out in the open, it becomes their business too.

After discovery, either by the lover's wife or mistress's husband, very few affairs continue. They might drag on for a few more weeks or months, but that is probably all unless some other aspect changes. Ultimately, either marriage, or both of them, might end, in which case, in theory, the relationship could carry on; otherwise, eventually, either party, or both of them will end the affair. Unless the lovers have open marriages, it is almost impossible to sustain an affair when one or more of the injured parties knows about it. Home life becomes unbearable.

The biggest problem for the married mistress, if the affair does end, is that she must go back whence she came. She returns to the same marriage with the same deficiencies that caused her to stray in the first place. Often her dissatisfaction has increased with the comparisons that she has begun, and will continue, to make between lover and husband. If the husband knows about the affair, he will have changed too and seldom for the better. The loss of her lover might disrupt her sense of identity and will affect her day-to-day living profoundly. He has probably provided her with most of her hope, love and excitement for the duration of the affair; these feelings are dashed, in one fell swoop, when he leaves.

If her affair has convinced her that her marriage is good and valuable, she is one of the lucky ones. Some women do find that an affair makes them appreciate what they have at home and others say that their affairs helped to improve their marriages and in particular, their sex lives. But for most this is not the case.

If the affair escaped detection, hers is probably one of the best-guarded secrets in the world and one that she keeps with considerable guilt. Despite the fact that her husband neither knows about nor suspects her infidelity, the fear of discovery does not stop with the end of the affair. She knows that at any time the truth could be discovered, and even if the relationship ended years before, the fact that it ever existed always presents a threat. Husbands are much less likely to end a marriage than wives, but this does not mean that they view infidelity any less seriously. In fact the opposite is likely to be the case.

With all the risks that the extramarital affair presents to married women, it is amazing that they ever happen at all and hardly surprising that most are short-lived. Yet despite the risks, there are still women who will sacrifice all that they have to follow the man they love, or believe they love. However, most married women only ever do this once. They are less likely to become serially unfaithful than men, since most do not see infidelity as the long-term solution to their problems.

If it really is that bad at home, they will, as the divorce statistics show, more often than their male counterparts, just pack their bags and leave.

7 The Wife, Family and Friends

We cannot over-emphasize the tremendous effect that your lover's immediate and extended family and friends and colleagues have upon both his attitude to you and to his relationship with you. It is a common mistake to consider only your lover's wife as your rival, whereas in reality the list also includes his children; his parents, brothers and sisters; his wife's family; his bosses at work and all his close acquaintances. Each separate group of individuals, he perceives, looks for different things from him and he works constantly to meet the considerable range of requirements they present.

This chapter examines the roles your lover is expected to play, the pressures he has to face and the ways in which all the people in his life affect his behaviour and the management of your affair.

Two basic principles underlie our general attitude to the state of matrimony. The first is that once you are married you are meant to stay married, and the second is that once you have children you are supposed to take care of them. Adultery, although nominally condemned, is often accepted reluctantly but only if it does not compromise these two basic principles. This is what underpins each lover's attitude to his affair.

Some men do leave their wives, but the man who takes a mistress is clearly not intending to be one of them. There is no reason, looked at dispassionately, why he should leave, since his mistress stays with him anyway. Whether he loves his wife or not, or whether he has considered leaving her for his mistress or not, are both irrelevant. The most important influences on him are the public and private roles he plays within his marriage.

Marriage is a bond that extends far beyond any romantic notions we may have about love. Each lover is used to being part of a couple, he gets used to being seen as both a husband and a father, used to the familiar reassurance of a known environment – no matter how unsatisfying at times. These men are seldom comfortable with change and, perhaps more importantly, are acutely aware of their public images. They want to be seen as successful in all that they do. Most, though not all, have a very keen sense of responsibility for their wives and children and believe they must maintain the family unit no matter what. Their mistresses are allowable only if they do not overtly threaten this unit.

All that a mistress knows of her lover's life is what he tells her. She sees only the tip of the iceberg that represents his responsibilities, hopes and dreams; as for the rest, she can only guess. Normally, once the lover–mistress relationship has been established, the lover will present his home life in a reasonably positive vein. He feels free to talk about his day-to-day activities and seldom discerns any conflict between his two distinct lives: both are established in his mind's eye; both are separate.

The vast majority of extramarital affairs are not discovered. If this was not the case, the divorce rate would most likely be even higher than it is at present. The vast majority of affairs are short-lived, thereby lessening the risk of detection. When a man takes a mistress this presents a completely different set of circumstances to the simple affair and the risk of detection is correspondingly greater. This is either because of simple probabilities – the increased number of meet- ings – or because the lover, in his familiarity with his situation, might become careless. At the point of detection, should it ever happen, his wife's reaction will invariably determine the future course of the affair. Until that time, her influence is often cloudy.

Throughout the relationship with her lover, the mistress wonders about his home life: what happens behind those closed doors and why does he stay with his wife? She supposes, or tries to convince herself, that his marriage must be unhappy – otherwise why would he need a mistress? She presumes there are flaws in his relationship with his wife. Neither of these speculations is necessarily true but, even if they are (and perhaps especially if they are) the very presence of the mistress makes it easier for him to stay rather than to leave. Friction at home is rendered more tolerable if he can remind himself that he will soon be with another woman who quite obviously adores him.

Each mistress fears her lover's wife in different ways and, as a direct result, is prone to taking a negative attitude to the wife's character and hold over her husband. Many mistresses criticize their rivals and believe that their lovers' wives are deficient in providing for their husbands' needs. More often than not, the mistress's view is incorrect. The lover is not necessarily being neglected at home; he is not necessarily unhappy there; nor need his wife be the villain or termagant the mistress hopes she may be. Yet each mistress knows that the future of her affair is threatened by her lover's wife's very presence and this is enough to tempt her to find ways to denigrate her. The mistress wants to believe that her lover's marriage is lacking and that this is his wife's fault, but the truth is rarely so simple. By thinking in this way, she helps to sustain the only hope she has, that one day he will see the light and leave home. It's a false and destructive hope.

Conversely, the wife will often place the blame for her husband's extramarital activities on the mistress and her inherent immorality. She sees the mistress as a woman who wants to steal her husband and who will stop at nothing in her attempts to succeed. This is sometimes true, but not always.

The film *Fatal Attraction* created a crude pastiche of the evil mistress and the victim wife, but, although it dealt in caricatures, the movie nevertheless made some interesting points. The 'other woman' was supposed to accept her rejection and not react or make a fuss. The fact that she reacted in a frenzy of jealous violence meant that the point, that perhaps she did have a right to feel used and abused, was lost. The film-makers' sympathies lay wholly with the man and his family, the only innocent party. We need to remind ourselves that *Fatal Attraction* is after all a manipulative fiction: most mistresses would not dream of disrupting their lovers' home lives. Women involved in a casual affair might be tempted to do so, but the long-standing mistress loves her man and often has to accept that his family is a part of who and what he is.

It is not clear why the husband/lover is not blamed in the same way as the wife and mistress. Perhaps it is easier for the women in his life to believe that he has been manipulated in some way rather than accept that his behaviour is entirely self-determined.

To understand fully all the reasons why a lover does not abandon his marriage, we need to look at the nature of all the relationships in his life, created both before and since his marriage. These include not only the relationship with his wife but also those with his children, his extended family and his friends.

First, we need to consider the lover's wife since she is the most obvious, and seemingly major, rival for his affections. If she so chooses, the ways in which she could oppose his mistress are many, provided she realizes that the mistress exists in the first place. Those mistresses we talked to, who believed their lovers' wives to be ignorant of the affair, expressed surprise that they had not guessed. They believed that the clues must after all be manifold. Unexplained or more frequent absences, different coloured hairs on his clothes, an unfamiliar perfume, changes in his behaviour (whether more or less attentive) and differences in his sexual needs or performance – all would indicate to the mistress that something was amiss and so she cannot understand how his wife fails to recognize the signs. Perhaps she does and chooses to ignore them; perhaps she is so remote from her husband that she is insensitive to the changes; perhaps she trusts him so much that the thought would never cross her mind; perhaps she does not care.

Wives of men who are unfaithful fall into one of three groups: those who do not know that their husbands are having an affair, those who suspect and those who know.

Those who genuinely do not know are more numerous than we would expect. This is attributable either to the lover's ability to lie or deceive convincingly, or to the fact that the thought of him being unfaithful would never cross his wife's mind. Much depends on the character of his wife and the extent to which she is either by nature suspicious or trusting. The lover will find the first type of wife hard to deceive in the long run, whereas the second is likely to view any warning signs as figments of her imagination, the thought of his infidelity being untenable.

Those who suspect live in a kind of limbo and most will strive to attain the truth, palatable or not. Some choose simply to ignore the situation. These women are hoping that if he is having an affair, it is a phase he is going through; they believe that if they continue ostrich-like, the affair will finally blow itself out. They are often proved right. Others, those with more courage, or perhaps with less artistry, might challenge their husbands by asking them outright whether their suspicions are justified. The husband might of course deny his infidelity, but he could also take this opportunity to confess. His wife's reaction will usually determine the path he takes.

However, the most interesting group by far are those wives who know. These can be further divided into those who knew from the outset, those who found out later but decided to say and do nothing, and finally those who found out and faced the issue head-on.

Wives who live as part of an open marriage not only know about their husbands' affairs but are likely to be told before the event. They accept these infidelities as a normal part of their marriage and have already taken, or are prepared to take, lovers of their own. They do not see sexual fidelity as an essential part of their marriages. This could indicate either that the couple are not truly in love, but maintain the marriage for more mercenary reasons; or that they are in love and bestowing sexual freedom is merely an expression of their particular kind of love. Such couples often maintain that they tell each other about their affairs because they value honesty within the marriage more than fidelity.

In theory, at least, the wife in an open marriage will not try to stop her husband's affair since it is pre-defined as a natural part of their relationship. Usually, however, neither party ever expects the other's affairs to become serious enough to threaten their marriage. This is the major danger for the open marriage, since affairs of the heart are notoriously difficult to contain and love for a third party is sometimes impossible to exclude.

Some couples maintain that if their partners do fall in love with someone else and want to leave, they will not prevent them from going. This is presented as an extension of the patterns of freedom and honesty established. However, hypothetical speculations are one thing; it is difficult to predict what would really happen if the rejected partner realized that his/her marriage was truly under threat. A mistress in this situation might be forgiven for believing that she has a better opportunity for a permanent relationship with her lover, but her lover's wife might surprise her when it comes to the crunch. She might, of course, let her husband go with her blessing, but she might also decide to fight. If she chooses the latter, she will have to be ingenious if she wants to maintain the premise of allowing her husband his freedom.

In open marriages, the wife represents a very different kind of adversary. There is no need to consider what might happen if she finds out about her husband's affair, because she already knows. There is little chance, in theory, that he might be compelled to leave by his wife's reaction. The husband has no need, in theory, to lie about his affair and, perhaps more importantly, he knows, in theory, that he has a well-defined safety net to catch him if the affair should end.

To the mistress, however, his wife presents a greater threat, because her husband will not expect her to launch an attack on his affair. The element of surprise is all hers. Because he believes completely in the implicit contract of the open marriage, his wife is free to act with virtual impunity. She could ask him to stop the affair. He could react in one of two ways, depending on how genuinely happy he is with the operation of his open marriage. He could reaffirm the terms of the agreement and refuse; or he could be pleased to find out that his wife can indeed get jealous and be relieved to abandon the precepts of an open marriage. The latter outcome is the most likely.

On the other hand, his wife could be more subtle. She knows him well and can therefore work on him; she has more time with him than his mistress and more time to win him back. He need never really know what her motivations are. A mistress we interviewed who found herself in such a situation was told by her lover that his wife appeared to be depressed. She wandered around the house and showed little interest in either herself or her social life. Her husband rightly became concerned. Within a few months he had left his mistress. Within six months, his wife had found another lover of her own and the open marriage was resumed at her instigation.

The most usual way for the affair to be discovered is that the lover's wife guesses, confronts him and then he confesses. The discovery will normally signal the end of the affair since she is most unlikely to want it to continue. She may issue an ultimatum, 'her or me', if she feels confident about her marriage, or she may throw him out. In all cases, however, she will be devastated by hurt and humiliation. Her pain alone, and his ensuing guilt, is often enough to cause the errant husband to abandon his affair. The pain caused to his wife can stem from a number of sources. Few betrayed wives say that the sexual element of the relationship was their predominant concern; many say that what hurts most is the deception involved; but the majority find the thought of the emotional and mental closeness between their husbands and mistresses the most difficult aspect to accept. If she is wise, she will know that he has talked to his mistress about his home life, and she will know that his mistress knows more about her than she knows about the mistress.

It is curious that our laws recognize adultery, the sexual aspect of an illicit relationship, as being a valid reason for divorce, whereas, in fact, the most damaging feature is the emotional and mental bonding. Many wives say that they could accept a one-night stand, albeit reluctantly, but the concept of a parallel relationship is not acceptable. Even those who say that they find the one-night stand almost impossible to understand and wonder why their husbands would risk their marriages for something so trivial, would rather this than discover a long-standing deception.

When, or if, the lover's wife finds out, her condemnation of the mistress will far outweigh her condemnation of her husband and, should the two ever meet, she will be a dangerous adversary to face. It is easier for her to blame the woman for luring her husband away than to accept that he probably went of his own free will. In targeting the mistress, she hopes to convince herself that her marriage is really secure after all and that any man would have difficulty in resisting the wiles of such a woman. Other wives might take a completely different tack and start to blame themselves. Whatever the wife's reaction, her attitude to both her marriage and her husband will be changed forever. Most find the infidelity impossible to forget, even if they do eventually manage to forgive. The lover will not escape unscathed, but if his wife still loves him and neither is looking for a way out, he can often persuade her to allow him to stay.

In a very few situations, the lover might state his determination to continue to see his mistress or lie about his intention to end the relationship with her, but both these outcomes are rare. However, whatever happens, if his wife believes she might lose him and wants to keep him, she has a variety of options at her disposal.

If the lover's wife knows about his mistress, but has not yet revealed her knowledge to her husband, she is likely to pass through a number of stages. Her initial reaction of anger and pain is usually followed by a damaging period of self-blame, which is followed in turn by a determination to win him back. But even if she does subsequently threaten him with divorce, he is far more likely to find reasons why she should let him stay than run to the arms of his mistress.

She holds so many aces that it is difficult to know exactly where to start. First, she has time on her side. For whatever reasons, he has spent (and will continue to spend) much more time with her than with his mistress. She might try to win back his affection by changing her behaviour. She might decide not to confront him but to change the way she relates to him. She might make an effort to enhance their sex life, she might alter her appearance, she might treat him more attentively. It is possible that the marriage had gradually deteriorated, as most marriages do from time to time, and the discovery of the mistress could inject the sense of urgency needed to bring it back to life. As a result, the lover might rediscover the magic of his marriage and the mistress would no longer be necessary.

The lover and his wife have shared many experiences, both good and bad, and have a history – a photograph album of memories – which will help to bind them together. Even if he feels he no longer loves her, they are united by much more than passion. Mundane as some of these things may be, they form the basic elements that hold two people together. They have seen each other at their best and at their worst. She knows all his bad habits and she will have berated him often for his behaviour. Significantly, many husbands take pride in describing their wives' tirades and the implication that they rule the roost. It is almost like a conspiracy of compliance which, like the mason's handshake and apron, binds these men together in their collective experience of matrimony. On the other hand, they would never boast about such treatment from their mistresses. Mistresses are portrayed as beneficial and complementary to the man's way of life – there is obviously no kudos in being berated and nagged by one's mistress.

He behaves differently when he is with his wife than when he is with his mistress. In the marriage, the lines of control are established. Some aspects of the marriage are the wife's domain, some the husband's. It does not really matter how the division of labour has been allocated; demarcation lines have been drawn and both know their functions. With his mistress, almost without exception, he is in control and he makes most of the decisions. She is his caviar, his wife his daily bread; the former a luxury, the latter a necessity. When there are problems at home, he has to return to sort them out; when there are problems with his mistress, he can leave. When forced to look realistically at his situation, he can convince himself with ease that his relationship with his wife is real, whereas that with his mistress is fantasy.

He will tell himself that whereas his wife knows the real him and accepts him, his mistress would probably lose interest if she knew him as well as his wife. We have interviewed several mistresses who said that their lovers often remarked that if they were together all the time, their mistresses would not like them or become bored. They seem to believe that their mistresses would not tolerate the 'real them' in the same way as their wives. Their wives have shared the mundane, the difficult, the boring and the repetitive and they are still there. Their mistresses have not yet been put to this test and each lover suspects that his mistress would not accept the complete package. The lover's affair excites him, for he can behave in ways he would never dare at home and he can indulge his fantasies. He believes that his mistress sees most of his best and that she would leave him if she saw the man behind the mask. In fact, the mistress generally sees much more of what he is like than he cares to believe. However, some mistresses, especially wanton mistresses, probably would leave him if the excitement waned since no love binds them together. As for the rest, we really do not know – few lovers ever have the courage to put this theory to the test.

Each wife also has society on her side. She holds the ace called 'responsibility'. If he were ever to consider walking away from her, he knows that most people would condemn him. He would feel that he had failed and would expect others to view him in the same light. The longer the marriage, the more damning the condemnation. It is supposed that, having been married for so many years and having invested so much time in the relationship, it would be an absurd waste to throw it all away.

The ace of 'children' is also in his wife's hand. Even if a wife realizes that her husband no longer wishes to stay with her, she can, and sometimes will, use their children as a lever to make him stay or, at least, to increase his guilt. If 'How could you possibly leave me?' does not work, the trump of 'How could you possibly leave the children?' can be devastatingly effective. Even if she does not use her trump card, her husband knows it is there and finds the question almost impossible to answer.

Although there will always be exceptions, the love and responsibility that men feel towards their children, perhaps not publicized as much as mother love, is deep and significant. After separation, he knows that young children will certainly remain with their mother, and being the most obvious guilty party, he could easily lose the respect of older children. Both these realizations are often enough to make him stop to reconsider. Several men who leave their wives never see their children again; others never manage to re-establish good relationships with their children and that is an enormous price to pay. Even men who have stopped loving their wives seldom stop loving their children.

Then there is the threat of divorce. The lover knows that his home and assets are at risk if his wife chooses to divorce him. Although most wives suffer considerably after a separation, they can also, aided and abetted by the legal profession, exert incredible financial pressures on their husbands. They may be able to take half, if not more, of the joint assets. If a husband has paid for most of these assets, he will normally subconsciously view them as belonging to him, and the potential monetary losses are often enough to make him think twice. The richer the husband, the more he has to lose. If his wife is clever or bitter or both, she will make sure that he loses quite a lot!

No one would blame the lover's wife for trying to hold on to her husband. She has in all probability invested years of her life building her life with him; she has weathered the inevitable storms in any long-term relationship; she has put up with his unpleasant traits; and she has made a significant contribution to the man he has now become. Both he and their life together represent, in part, an investment for her future. Whether she loves him or not, she probably wants to keep him and is likely to fight anyone who challenges her with everything at her disposal. The only exceptions are those wives who, for whatever reason, do not feel that strongly about preserving their marriages, or those rare women who would rather see their partners leave than hold them to a relationship they no longer appear to want.

The relationship between parents and their children is complex and involves a number of mutual dependencies. From studies that have examined the effect of divorce on children of all ages conflicting conclusions emerge. Some suggest that divorce is always detrimental, others that it is better for a child to be raised by one parent than in an unhappy marriage. However, there have been no studies on the effects of affairs on children.

Without detailed analysis, it is impossible for us to establish all the effects of affairs on children, but we did speak to a number of adults who can remember incidents from their childhood. From what they could recall, their reactions appeared to vary depending upon their age at the time. The very young were not bothered one way or another provided their parents continued to reassure them; teenagers tended not to take it too seriously, finding embarrassment to be the most painful problem they had to deal with. Other children, those who had begun to view their parents as people in their own right rather than appendages, reacted according to the relationship they had established with each parent. Some, but very few, were even told about the affairs while they were happening. It appears that the discovery of an infidelity has considerably less impact on children than divorce. However, our small sample cannot be used as absolute proof of this but it does appear that children will be as upset as the parents want them to be.

When young, children are dependent upon their parents for their physical, mental and emotional sustenance and these dependencies form the basis for the close family bond. The man, usually the major breadwinner, feels most of the responsibility for their subsistence. In their early years, much of the direct nurturing comes from the mother and some of the earliest emotional and physical bonds are formed with her. All children are acutely sensitive to their surroundings and will register instinctively any changes that may occur. They see their environment, no matter how strange, as how the world must be; this represents their normality. Therefore they will be disturbed by friction between mother and father caused by an extramarital affair only when it causes noticeable changes to the status quo. Unless the problems are so great that divorce becomes imminent, parents are extremely unlikely to tell younger children about their problems, but this does not mean that they will not detect any deterioration in their parents' relationship.

Dependency is not a one-way street; many parents become dependent upon their children, especially in those situations in which the relationship between father and mother is strained. Children can easily become the focus for the marriage and the reason for its perpetuation. This is seen by society as both an admirable and a valid way to behave.

In addition, the easily given love and trust of children can often compensate for the lack of closeness in a marriage, thereby making them doubly important.

Children need a stable home life and the protection of preferably both parents. Usually the lover with children will do everything in his power to protect them from his infidelity even if it is discovered. He will worry about his wife using the children against him, and about losing their love and respect. He might feel that his affair has little to do with his home life and he definitely does not want it to affect his children adversely. Some lovers we have spoken to, whose relationships with both their mistresses and their older children are particularly close, have thought about bringing them together. Fortunately, this thought is seldom put into action, except perhaps in countries like France, where liaisons with mistresses are more open and acceptable. Typically, if a lover tried to do such a thing, and his wife was to find out, she would consider the mistress as a threat not only to her marriage but also to her relationship with her children. Mothers defending their young are fierce opponents, and it would be an unwise man who took this risk.

Lovers interviewed by us have recounted situations in which wives have deliberately used children as a way of pressurizing their husbands to stay in their marriages. Lovers who have left home have either been denied access or else their wives have found a way to block previously planned visits. Sometimes the husband's parents are contacted by his wife to add to the pressure and to remind him of his family responsibilities.

Often, as a direct result, the lover will stay or will feel compelled to return. If he returns, he comes back not because he realizes he loves his wife more than he thought, but because he cannot live with the guilt of abandoning his children. The wife in these situations does not care that he has not returned for her sake; it is enough that he came back. For those marriages that subsequently survived (as most do), each lover said with hindsight that he believes that he did the right thing, mostly because he honoured his responsibilities – responsibilities that had been instilled in him by his own parents and his upbringing. Love found elsewhere is seen as no excuse to abandon a marriage and especially the children of the union, and lack of love does not make that marriage invalid. Most people would see the lover's return to the fold as the right and admirable thing to do.

In these situations the children are often told about the infidelity by their mothers, sometimes many years after the event. If they were young when the trauma occurred, they tend not to recall it at all and are seldom bothered by it later, provided their parents are together and appear to have made a success of their marriage. Such children seem to view the episode with a degree of amusement and probably find it difficult to believe that their old dad actually managed to be indiscreet in his youth.

If the lover's parents are still alive, they too can cause him considerable difficulties, especially if they like his wife. All parents tend to take pride in their children's achievements and take most, or at least some, of the blame for their failures. The lover's parents are no different. Unless the lover is particularly close to his parents, he is unlikely to tell them about his mistress. They will usually discover his infidelity only once his wife finds out, and perhaps not even then.

Many parents see problems in their children's marriages as a personal reflection on themselves and the quality of their parenting. They are also marginally less tolerant of their sons' infidelities than of their daughters'. This has much to do with the commonly held, but limited, view that men are responsible and rational whereas women are led by their feelings. They might find it slightly more acceptable if their son had a casual affair, but it is quite a different matter if he becomes seriously involved with another woman.

Parents' attitudes may be slightly modified if they are no longer together. Divorced parents are sometimes more understanding of the conflict between emotional needs versus the demands of duty. Despite this, parents do not want to see their children's marriages fail and will try their best to ensure that all options are explored before supporting any separation. The man's parents, in particular, will also be concerned about losing contact with their grandchildren, and all parents worry about their children's pain no matter how old those children are.

Most parents believe that they have brought up their children to be responsible and will want this sense of responsibility to override all else. They also want their children to be happy and will therefore give the most positive and protective advice they can. They will want the best for their son and, for most, this means urging him to stay with, and work at, his marriage. They will usually maintain that since they managed to stay together, he should endeavour to do the same, for all concerned. He knows full well what they expect of him and he will feel as if he is failing them.

If his parents are still married, they are likely to tell him that marriage does not sustain passion forever, that it is transitory and will always fade to be replaced by a different kind of love and commitment. They will expect him to accept that his current marriage, probably not unlike their own, is the best he could hope for and imply that, over time, his relationship with his mistress would evolve in the same way. However, in most cases, if he does leave, his parents, in the way of all parents, will still be there to support him whether they agree with his decision or not.

His wife's parents, naturally, will support their daughter and are likely to bear a grudge against her husband long after his wife has forgiven him, assuming that she ever does. The closer he is to both his own parents and siblings, and to his wife's family, the worse he will feel about letting them down. It is a fact that almost no one will support the lover and he will feel the need to justify himself to everyone. For the man in this predicament, faced with all this condemnation, all the people who tell him he is wrong, love alone looks like a pretty feeble excuse for ending his marriage. What if they are all right? What if, having left his wife, his children, damaged his relationship with his parents; what if, after doing all this, the relationship with his mistress does not work?

The risks he perceives are enormous and start to erode his faith in his love for his mistress. If he can no longer persuade himself that he can live his dual life forever, if he has to choose, all the advice he is receiving, all his logic, will be heavily weighted in his wife's favour.

Finally, we must consider his friends and work colleagues. His friends, unless they have been through the same turmoil, will probably encourage him in his exploits with his mistress, but will continually remind him that he should take care not to damage his marriage. Even if they have met his mistress and like her, they are far more likely to caution him on being careful than to encourage him to consider leaving home.

The lover probably has few male friends with whom he can share the intimate details of his affair and the emotional and mental problems he is experiencing. He may not hide his affair, but he will seldom be inclined to air his vulnerabilities and sensitivities. In short, unless he has close female friends, he probably has few people he can talk to and who could help him to think through his options. Therefore, most of his decisions he makes on his own – decisions that will be based upon the generally accepted precepts about extramarital affairs. In this context, he is likely to conclude that the most logical and acceptable option is for him to stay married.

At work the situation is difficult to assess; much depends on his status and the attitude of his company. Generally speaking, the more important his role and the higher his company profile, the less likely his superiors are to tolerate emotional indiscretions – even in his private life. Some companies have unwritten rules that their executives must be married; some companies even interview wives before filling senior positions. If the lover is having an affair with a colleague, the situation can be doubly damning. First, it is often seen as unprofessional behaviour and second, it is possible that many of his colleagues know his wife, thereby increasing the risk of exposure and lessening their respect for him. It is conceivable that his company bosses would intervene in his relationship with his mistress by changing his job (or, more likely, his mistress's job). We have been told of situations in which one or both of the parties have been sacked once their affair was made public and others where the participants were moved to new locations. We know of another scenario in which a lover's wife, having discovered her husband was having an affair with someone at work, called his boss to complain. He was moved to a new part of the company. An affair, therefore, potentially threatens the lover's career as well as his home life.

Most of the situations we have outlined above address what might happen once the affair is discovered. However, even if the affair is not detected, in his mind's eye the lover is aware of all these possible eventualities. They are what keep him within the marriage and what cause him to guard his secret with care. Significantly, they are often what prompt him to take a mistress in the first place, indulging in romantic fantasy rather than facing confrontation at home. He is only too aware of his wife's potential reaction; he is aware of the possible threat to his relationships with his children and his parents; he is aware of the possible risks to his career, he is aware of the costs and pains of divorce. If his mistress really does want him to leave home, she does not just have to be better than his wife; she has to be worth him losing his children, his parents, his prestige and his money too. The arguments against are overwhelming, and if we are honest, it is obvious why, in the vast majority of cases, the mistress will always lose.

8 Legal and Financial Considerations

If you are a reluctant mistress, you have probably not thought much about your legal position in the relationship, unless, of course, you work in the profession. It might seem unimportant at present, but understanding what rights and expectations you have, if any, and whether your expectations are realistic, might affect your future decisions.

Everyone needs to make financial provision for the future, but if you intend to remain a mistress it is especially important. You need to plan for the worst case scenario, for example that you will have to rely upon your own resources if you have an accident, serious illness, if you become unemployed and, of course, when you retire. It is wisest to assume that you will not get any financial support from your lover. As a mistress, you have no entitlement to maintenance, his pension or a share of his estate.

The first part of this chapter explores the mistress's legal position in the light of current family and property law and a range of other provisions relevant to those whose relationship exists outside marriage. It is a broad layperson's guide, and by no means exhaustive. The mistress is strongly advised to seek the advice of a professional if she wants to ascertain the legal position with respect to her own circumstances.

In the second part of the chapter we discuss what types of financial provision the mistress should consider making for herself. The discussion is general, because only accredited financial advisers are legally permitted to make recommendations on financial investments and therefore no reference is made to any particular providers.

The Legal Position

It is a popular fallacy that if a woman lives with a man she automatically gains the same financial and property rights and benefits as her married counterparts. In fact the concept of a 'common law' spouse under English law has not existed since Lord Hardwicke's Act in 1753. The mistress does not usually share a home or live with her lover, but even if she did that would not in itself give her any greater financial rights of her own. In the eyes of the law, she is just a girlfriend and has no rights against her lover *per se*. There are numerous cases reported which show just how unfair and illogical the current law appears to be, which is why our advice is that the mistress should make her own provisions for the future from the outset.

Briefly, as the law currently stands, financial provision under statute for unmarried partners is limited to claims by engaged couples to determine existing property rights; claims for inheritance when the other cohabitant dies; and claims for children of cohabitants. There is no other legislation on which cohabitants or mistresses/lovers may rely which allows the court to divide assets between them as it thinks fair, no matter how long the relationship has been established or however deserving the claimant. In the absence of legislation governing property rights, recourse has to be made to common law and equitable principles. Cohabitants and mistresses (and lovers) are in an equal position although cohabitants might in practice be more successful with property claims. Furthermore, there is no legal obligation of support between cohabitants.

By way of illustration, let us look at the cases of Mrs Burns,[1] Miss Mitchell[2] and Ms Smith.[3]

Mrs Burns lived with her male partner for nineteen years bearing and bringing up their two children. She changed her name by deed poll, and her friends and acquaintances believed they were married. She paid the rates, the telephone bills, purchased items for the house and redecorated the interior. However, she did not contribute either to the purchase price or to the mortgage. When the relationship ended, the Court of Appeal held that her contribution to the welfare of the family by performing the domestic duties and bringing up the children was not sufficient to entitle her to a share of the property.

In the case of Ms Smith, her lover had maintained her and their daughter in a separate property for years and, when she asked him to put the house into joint names, he replied to the effect: 'Don't worry. I have told you I will always look after you.' Her claim to keep the property, or even the right to continued occupancy until their daughter was seventeen years old, failed.

Miss Mitchell lived with her lover, who made representations about their future together, talking of them being engaged and saying that as soon as he was divorced they would marry. He made what were held to be invalid excuses as to why the property they bought together was in his sole name (citing tax relief and protecting his assets against his former wife's claims). He talked of the property being shared equally with her. The court held that she was entitled to an equal beneficial share partly as a result of these discussions between them which in the court's view amounted to an understanding that the property should be shared equally.

Had Mrs Burns or Ms Smith been married they would have had a claim to a share of the property on divorce regardless of financial contribution. Miss Mitchell on the other hand was entitled to receive her half share merely on account of the discussions with her lover, which seems unfair when compared with the situations of Mrs Burns and Ms Smith.

However, the law would appear to be fair as between the sexes: had Mrs Burns been the sole owner of the property it is highly unlikely that her male partner would have been granted any share either. As an example, in the case of Thomas v. Fuller-Brown,[4] the boyfriend was unsuccessful in his claim of a share in the property despite having carried out a major renovation including design and construction of a two-storey extension, rebuilding the kitchen and landscaping the garden.

Although the injustices suffered by the likes of Mrs Burns are all too apparent, the courts have repeatedly made the point that regrettably, any change is a matter for Parliament. Let us therefore look in more detail at how mistresses are positioned in terms of property and inheritance claims, and provision for children before commenting on difficulties faced by prospective law reformers.

Claims regarding property

In the event of a breakdown of the relationship, a mistress can only claim against the property which her lover has provided for her or which she has acquired together with him. Where title documentation is inconclusive as to ownership and in the absence of any agreement between the parties, claims in respect of property must be dealt with by reference to a combination of property and trust law. A vast amount of complex and technical case law governs the sorts of claims that may be made. Given the uncertainties in this area, any litigation required to establish an interest in property is likely to be emotional, time consuming and expensive.

There are three equitable rights which a mistress might seek to establish: resulting trust; constructive trust; and proprietary estoppel.

A resulting trust might arise where property is purchased in the name of a person who has contributed only in part, or not at all, to the purchase price. In that circumstance it is presumed that there is a common intention that the legal owner holds the other party's share on trust in an amount proportionate to that which he or she contributed. In the absence of written or other corroborative evidence, assuming that the fact of contribution has been proved, the onus would be upon the legal owner to rebut the claim that this was the common intention and that the contribution was made.

A constructive trust may be established in one of two ways. Both have the same effect. First, there are cases where there is evidence of express discussions between the parties during which they have agreed to share the beneficial interest in the property. Second, there are cases where, although there is no evidence of an express agreement, the court is able to infer a common intention by reference to the conduct of the parties involved. The test for establishing a constructive trust is very strict and falls into two parts. The first part is that there must be evidence of a common intention that both parties would have an interest in the property. That common intention might be proven by evidence of an express agreement or, in the absence of this, by inference from conduct. It has been held in a case decided by the House of Lords that direct contributions to the purchase price by the partner who is not the legal owner, either initially or by payment of mortgage instalments, will justify the inference necessary for the creation of a constructive trust but that it is at least extremely doubtful whether anything less will do[5]. The second part of the test is that the non-owning party has acted to his or her detriment or has significantly altered his/her position by relying on the common intention.

In the case of Mrs Burns, the house was in the man's name and as she made no financial contribution either to the purchase price, deposit or the mortgage payments she was not entitled to any share of the property. Maintaining the house, meeting household expenditure and looking after their children for seventeen years was not seen as a common intention for her to have a beneficial interest in the house. In the case of Miss Mitchell, there was seen to be an express agreement as the lover had promised to share the property equally and she had relied to her detriment on that common intention.

An alternative principle (established by Lord Denning) but one that is rarely used is that of primary estoppel. This is where the claimant has to establish that there was an assurance or promise by the owner of the property which the claimant relies on to his or her detriment. An example of this is the case of Wayling v. Jones,[6] where the court awarded the non-owning party the proceeds of the sale of the hotel which it was held he had been promised and where, in reliance on that promise, he had acted to his detriment by working for virtually no pay. Where a person is not seeking an interest in the property but simply a right to continue to occupy a property based on a promise, the technical term is 'licence by estoppel'. However, the same rules as those for detriment apply. In the previously commented case of Ms Smith, where the lover had simply promised to take care of her, always, her claim failed because it was held that she had not acted to her detriment. Her actions in leaving her husband, becoming pregnant, bringing up their child and refraining from getting any job was not seen as stemming from any reliance on a promise.

In light of all of the above, let us therefore consider the situation where the mistress is either provided with a property by the lover or acquires a property with him. She can simply accept the offer with the understanding that she has no legal rights to that property, unless there is an express agreement between them to that effect. Even then, she would be well advised to make financial contributions, as she is able, either to the deposit, legal costs, purchase price or the mortgage, in the form of instalments or lump sums. As the law presently stands any financial contributions in terms of home making, looking after the children, paying for the property upkeep or any other property-related outgoings will not be taken into account when establishing whether she has a beneficial interest. An anomaly of the law is that once a beneficial interest has been established these sorts of factors might be considered when quantifying the extent of her share.[7] Lastly, she must not rely on any promise of 'I'll always look after you', unless the lover is willing to share the legal and beneficial ownership. Ideally, so as to avoid future uncertainty, when a lover purchases a property for his mistress and it has been made clear to her that she should have an interest in this property even though she might not be registered on the legal title, it is important that she and her lover enter into a declaration of trust setting out their respective beneficial interests. The terms of such an agreement can also cover other practical issues such as the liability of each of the parties with respect to mortgage instalments and other ongoing items of expenditure if the relationship breaks down.

Claims by engaged couples

If there is an agreement to marry, then one or other of the parties can apply to the court under the Married Women's Property Act (1882, as amended) for a declaration as to their respective beneficial interest in the property. Such an application has to be made within three years of the termination of the agreement. There is no guidance in the statute as to what constitutes an 'agreement to marry' so in practice proving it can be difficult. It doesn't mean that there has to have been a 'formal' engagement. The judge will decide whether in his or her opinion the argument is valid. The agreement can of course be disputed easily by the other party, so trying to fulfil this requirement in order to use the procedure is tricky and could mean additional costs if the 'agreement to marry' is not accepted by the court. It is unclear whether a mistress could use this procedure as the lover is already married, but in principal it does apply to *all* agreements to marry. However, the court could argue that as the agreement could not be enforced, it is therefore invalid.

Claims regarding inheritance

When a cohabitant dies the other has a potential claim[8] if the parties have lived together as husband and wife in the same household for at least two years immediately prior to the date of the deceased's death. A surviving former cohabitant will, however, be ineligible to claim no matter how long the cohabitation if the relationship had ended prior to the death. Thus, Mrs Burns might have succeeded in her claim had her partner died instead of leaving her. As the mistress will rarely cohabit with the lover it is unlikely that she could claim under this provision. In any event she would also have to establish that the deceased was maintaining her, either wholly or in part, immediately before his death. Even if she satisfies those criteria, it is likely that she would still have to compete with other claimants.

With inheritance, the main beneficiaries are the deceased's family, as understood by the law. A surviving mistress has no rights under the rules governing intestacy. If the testator (who was married at the time of death) has died intestate (i.e. without a will), the surviving wife is absolutely entitled either to the entire estate (if there are no children or close relatives) or to a statutory legacy if there are children.[9] In many cases there is nothing left over after the legacy has been deducted from the estate.

If the estate has reverted to the crown, which will happen when there is no valid will or surviving immediate relations, the mistress can apply to the court for a provision to be made as a matter of grace.[10] Other cases where a mistress could apply for a provision of her lover's estate[11] are where his wife died before him or where she believes that she should be entitled to a provision based on the strength and circumstances of her relationship. In all of these cases, however, she must prove that she might 'reasonably expect' a provision from the deceased's estate. It is fair to say that these proceedings can be costly and the courts have limited powers.

Where the lover has made a will and intended to refer to the mistress but has not named her, it is not always possible for the court to act upon his wishes. There have been cases where a man has kept two households and left his estate to 'my wife during her widowhood', but naming the mistress. It is then up to the courts to decide what the testator's intention might have been. If the lover has made a provision for the mistress in his will identifying her by name, then she is obviously entitled to inherit. However, her legacy can still be contested by other qualified applicants such as the surviving spouse or even former spouse.[12]

Claims regarding inheritance for children

If the lover does not make any clear statement in his will to exclude his non-marital children from any interest, then the rights of succession are the same for all his natural children, providing that the will was made after 1969.[13] A later addition to the law[14] makes it possible for an illegitimate child to be an executor and qualify where the term 'heir' has been used in the will. In cases where the father's will has explicitly excluded a child who subsequently applies to the court, he or she can only qualify under the rules of having been maintained by the deceased. The objective of this is to ensure that while the child has a right to reasonable financial support from his deceased father, the father's rights to decide the beneficiaries of his estate should not be unnecessarily violated. This is different to the law in some other European countries where a minimum percentage of the estate is allocated to children, legitimate or not, which the parents cannot redistribute by making a will.

In cases of intestacy, a child of unmarried parents has rights of succession in respect of both his parents and remoter members of both paternal and maternal families,[15] as long as paternity has been legally proved or established by the father's acceptance. In relation to deaths occurring after 4 April 1988 the child retains the right to claim even if the property had already been distributed.[16] However, if the lover dies without leaving a will and was still married, and if the statutory legacy to his surviving wife exhausts the estate, the mistress's child might not receive anything. Whether or not a child of the deceased has received a bequest, he has the right to apply to the court under the provision as previously mentioned.

Claims regarding financial provision for children

It should be noted[17] that the court is empowered to make financial provision only for the benefit of the child/children and not for the mother *per se*. A mistress who has a child by her lover can claim financial provision only as the present carer of the child. The provision awarded by the court can take the form of periodical payments, lump sum orders or orders for the settlement or transfer of property.

In relation to maintenance, in general terms, in the absence of the parties reaching agreement on maintenance and unless one of the parties lives abroad, all claims for maintenance must be made through the Child Support Agency. The court only has jurisdiction to make an award for maintenance over and above the level ordered by the CSA provided that a full (not an interim) assessment has been completed by the agency.

Where the father can afford it, an order for a settlement of property is usually made, which in practice means that a property is transferred or purchased for the child/children to live until they reach 18. After that, the mother would have to find alternative accommodation. The court will take a number of factors into account in deciding what order if any should be made (including: income; earning capacity and other financial resources; financial needs; obligations and responsibilities of the applicant and the respondent to any claim; and the financial needs of the child).

By way of illustration, let us look at the cases of A v. A[18] and Phillips v. Peace.[19]

In the case of A v. A, the father was a very wealthy man who was resident outside the UK and used to visit the mother on an irregular basis. The mother alleged that he was the father of her three children and that they had been through a ceremony of marriage. It was subsequently found that he had only fathered one of the children and that the marriage had never taken place.

The court ordered that the property acquired by the father as a home for them would be settled on trust for the benefit of the 10-year-old child in question. The term of the trust was to terminate six months after the child attained the age of 18 or six months after she completed full-time education (to include tertiary education), whichever was the later. In terms of maintenance, the father was ordered to pay periodical payments to the child at the rate of £20,000 per annum and school fees and extra until 18, completion of her full-time education or further order.

In the case of Phillips v. Peace, the mother and father met in March 1993 and the relationship ended in September 1993. The father owned and controlled a company through which he carried on a business dealing in shares and lived in a house worth £2.6 million. The mother had pursued a career as a model and a singer, but by 1991 was in receipt of income support and housing benefit.

The mother sought a sum sufficient to enable her to buy a house or flat in central London for £350,000. The father suggested a figure of £75,000 for accommodation. An anomaly of this case was that the mother was not entitled to apply to the court for maintenance for the benefit of the child since the CSA had jurisdiction. However, notwithstanding the father's capital wealth, the CSA made a nil assessment because of his lack of income.

The court ordered the father to pay a lump sum of £90,000 to enable the mother to buy a house, plus £24,307.51 for furniture, costs in respect of the birth and other expenses. The mother and the child were to be entitled to live in the property until the child had grown up and completed her education. On schooling, the mother had applied for provision to enable the child to be privately educated, but Mr Justice Johnson said: 'This does not seem to me to be a case where at this stage I will make a provision for C on the basis of private education.'

In both cases the mother was allowed to live in the property only until the child attained the age of 18 or completed full-time education whichever the later. No maintenance order was made for the benefit of the mother, only of the child. In the case of Phillips v. Peace, even though the father was very wealthy, the order did not provide the child with a standard of living that she might expect to enjoy had she lived with her mother and father.

Domestic violence

Whilst we have discussed financial provision for unmarried couples there is one other form of statutory provision on which an unmarried person might rely: under the Family Law Act[20] one party might be able to oust the other from a shared property or obtain an order against non-molestation/harassment for a limited period of time. This is a complicated area of the law with strict qualifying criteria and the mistress should seek professional advice if she wishes to give consideration to taking such action.

Rented accommodation

If the mistress lives in rented accommodation as a joint tenant with the lover or if the tenancy is in the sole name of the lover, she is vulnerable to an action for possession regardless of whether or not he has actually resided in the property. Again, this is a complex area of the law, dependent on different Acts[21] relating to private sector accommodation, public sector housing and children. If the relationship ends she should seek professional advice and, ideally, seek to ensure that the tenancy is in her name alone from the outset.

Difficulties faced by prospective law reformers

Initially, relationships are based on mutual trust and good faith; very few couples prepare a pre-nuptial agreement before they marry, or a cohabitation agreement if they plan to live together. Similarly, most mistresses are unlikely to insist on a declaration of trust in cases where the lover provides her with a property and she will probably believe the lover's statements of 'always looking after her' or even his promise to marry her.

Those who marry and subsequently divorce might find, sometimes to their consternation, that the way in which assets are divided or redistributed by the court is dependent on a number of statutory factors. The settlement which is ultimately at the court's discretion is not decided by simply looking at the individual financial contributions or the length of the relationship. On the other hand, in a similar situation those who cohabit could find that they are left with nothing if the relationship ends. Those who only have an extramarital relationship are usually simply left out in the cold whether or not they have cohabited; their claim to any share of property, inheritance or maintenance is often a lost cause. Lastly, children born outside marriage cannot be guaranteed the same security as their legal counterparts.

The current legislation has a number of anomalies: there is greater protection for a cohabitant whose partner has died than there is for the one whose partner has walked away from the partnership. A financial contribution made by either party in the form of looking after the home or caring for the family might be taken into account when quantifying the share of an interest in a property but not in assessing whether that interest has or has not been established in the first place. All this raises many questions. Should cohabitants have the same rights and responsibilities as married couples, and should this apply to cohabitants of the same sex? How should mistresses or lovers be treated? Should the legislation be different if there are children from the union? How do you define the boundaries of these relationships? Should there be a threshold in terms of the duration of the cohabitation, and, in what circumstances should a person having a relationship with somebody married to another be considered to have financial, property or even inheritance rights? For example, in cases where a married man maintains a wife and their child in one and a mistress and their child in another, separate establishment, should these rights be shared between the two women? And if so, under which criteria?

The words of Nourse J. in the case of Grant v. Edwards[22]: 'the law is not so cynical as to infer that a woman will only go to live with a man to whom she is not married if she understands that she is to have an interest in their home. . .' seem reasonable but also pose the question of why her position should be any different to a woman who goes to live with a man she marries.

The Law Commission is in the process of reviewing the present law relating to unmarried couples. Clearly, the anomalies of the law are not simple to address. Any changes to the law present a fundamental problem of public policy regarding the institution of marriage. Other jurisdictions have addressed these issues differently. In Australia, the legislation[23] is sufficiently wide to cover both heterosexual and same sex relationships, and recognizes the contributions of cohabitants as homemaker and parent in a substantial manner irrespective of whether they have made a financial contribution.

New legislation in this area is long overdue and we must wait to see how any proposals for reform will redress the rights of cohabitants and those, who per definition do not cohabit, i.e. mistresses and lovers.

The Financial Position

In light of her legal position the mistress should not plan on receiving financial support from her lover during the relationship, on the breakdown of the relationship or after his death.

In financial planning, it is important that the mistress decides first and foremost what level of financial security and out-of-work income she requires in the short and long term. She may want to maintain her current standard of living, which might include financial contributions by the lover, or she might be content with less in her later years.

Be that as it may, she must acknowledge that in the face of the demographic changes and ensuing political pressures it is unlikely that state pensions or DSS benefits will be sufficient to secure a comfortable living by anybody's standards. Changes in legislation are bound to happen and, ideally, she should plan for her retirement as if the state pension did not exist. She should also discount any income or capital injection from the lover or his estate.

Unless she has independent means, she is probably working and therefore looking after her job prospects. Skills development and her career are important to her future well-being. She will also be more secure if she has a home of her own, and therefore this is one of the things she should focus upon. Even if the lover is paying her rental or contributing to her living expenses, she cannot rely on this continuing.

If the lover buys a property for her to live in then she should find out if he means her to share the ownership. If he does, then, as advised in the legal section, the mistress should make sure that her name is put on the title deeds, and execute a declaration of trust with percentage shares in which they hold the property. If she is contributing to the mortgage then this will make her later claim to the property stronger, but it is still important to legalize the share of the ownership. She should consult a lawyer to make sure that her entitlement is legally valid especially if she did not contribute financially at the outset. It might not be easy for the mistress to ask her lover to do this as she will probably feel that she should be grateful to him and not make demands, but there have been cases where this natural reluctance has caused the mistress to lose her home.

Even if accommodation is provided by her lover, the mistress should still consider buying her own, if she can afford to, and let it for the time she has no use for it. There are of course costs involved in letting a property, such as maintenance, but even if there is no surplus income it should still break even. The value of the property will eventually appreciate and she will have a home if and when she needs it.

If the mistress is single, she should also consider making provisions in case she loses her job, has an accident or becomes seriously ill. There is a wealth of different insurances available but the prices and conditions vary considerably, so it is important to shop around. It is not easy for the individual to find the best insurance as the market changes continuously and the products can be complex. Therefore, it is a good idea to consult two or three recognized independent financial advisers before making any decisions. The main types of insurance the mistress should consider are outlined below.

Income protection insurance is available from many insurance companies today and will pay a monthly income if she cannot work due to accident or illness. The level of the monthly payment can be chosen to match her needs, but will obviously be related to the level of her earned income.[24] She could also select a suitable 'waiting period', i.e. the time she has to wait before the monthly payments commence. This is usually anything from four weeks to twelve months, and would depend on her notice period and the length of fully paid sick leave that her employers will pay. The amount of the monthly insurance payment due is mainly dependent on the afore-mentioned parameters.[25] This insurance can pay out until her chosen retirement age, as long as she is unable to work.

If she has a mortgage, she can choose to take payment protection, which will usually pay her mortgage for twelve months of unemploy-ment or illness. The waiting period is one to three months. The lender will normally require life assurance if she has a repayment mortgage. If the mistress has no dependants, then it should be sufficient to take decreasing term assurance, which means that only the remaining debt of the mortgage will be paid on her death. This is cheaper than taking level term assurance on the total amount borrowed.[26] Critical illness cover can sometimes be included. In the case of an endowment mort-gage, the lender will similarly require a guaranteed life cover and crit-ical illness is again usually included (but at a premium). It could be argued that if the mistress has no dependants and does not wish to make any provisions then she does not necessarily need life assurance as the property is an asset that can be sold to cover the debt.

If she has children then she should consider full life cover and possi-bly also look at suitable investments to cover school fees or university expenses. Additional unemployment cover can be taken either sepa-rate from or together with the mortgage payment protection, depend-ing on the lender and the best offer available. Store cards and credit cards offer payment protection insurance as well, sometimes with illness cover and sometimes with unemployment cover only. It is worth considering whether to use this or to top up the income protec-tion and unemployment insurance to cover credit card payments if the cards are regularly used. It is also advisable to build up an emergency fund, covering normal expenses for a period of three to six months. This could be an ordinary building society account, perhaps giving a higher interest rate but immediate access to the funds when required.

All of the above may sound like a lot of expense, but the cost of these insurances is directly related to the income protection the mistress requires, which in turn is related to her normal level of earned income. As the mistress cannot rely on the lover, she should evaluate her financial position and at least make the provisions that she views are absolutely necessary and that she can afford. If the mistress lives alone she should make sure that somebody close to her knows what arrangements she has made or at least, where to find the necessary documents. Illness or accidents might involve stays in hospital and it can be difficult under the circumstances to remember to claim in time.

Finally the mistress should make sure that she has made reasonable pension arrangements. The government has made it more or less clear that nobody should expect the state pension to be adequate for retirement income, so this is not specific to mistresses. It is however an important part of her financial planning as she will have to take into account pension contributions along with her other outgoings if she has no spouse to support her.

If she has not been in continuous employment this will reduce her entitlement to the state pension. If she has stayed at home to raise a family, then she will not have any company pension for that period. For the time she was not working she has not been allowed to make personal pension arrangements and she might not benefit from her ex-husband's pension[27] either. Even if she has been in permanent full-time employment she should still consider a private pension.

Building a pension is expensive, and the later this begins the more expensive it is. Inland Revenue rules limit pension contributions to a percentage of the salary in order to claim tax relief. For example, people over 36 can put a maximum of 20% of their salary into their pension, and unused relief from the previous seven years can also be used. Returns on pension schemes are dependent on uncontrollable factors like interest rates, inflation and government policy, as well as the company's skill in investing the contributions. Personal pensions have been heavily criticized for heavy charges which include large commissions to salesmen, both of which reduce the growth rate.

It is almost impossible to guarantee that a pension plan will be adequate, as thousands of dissatisfied personal pension holders know to their cost. A 40-year-old earning the national average salary of £18,000 would expect to retire on a pension of two thirds of final salary at 60. If we assume that she had not made any previous contributions, this is her only pension plan, the investment grows at 9% a year,[28] and her salary by 3%, then she would have to pay £474 gross per month to achieve this. This means that her final salary would be £32,000, and her annual pension £21,300. The tax relief at 24% means that the actual net payment per month would be £360. A 45-year-old in the same circumstances would have to pay £699 gross or £531 net of tax per month. This means that the 45-year-old will be paying £171 or 47.5% more per month in comparison to the 40-year-old.[29]

Pensions can be bought over the telephone from direct pension companies or by contacting an independent or tied financial adviser. It is worth listening to a number of people, including friends, in an effort to grasp at least the basics, before biting the bullet. The pension plans will often be presented with three different interest rates, and it is best to err on the side of caution and look at the smallest return. Charges levied by the insurance company can affect the return by nearly one per cent a year, and they can be levied right at the beginning of the plan or in stages, and this has an effect on the growth of the investment. The growth projections may look fine, but the value or purchasing power of future money will be less than today, and the problem is that nobody knows by how much.

Financial planning is hardly something that most of us enjoy, but for single women and especially mistresses who decide to stay in the relationship this is a must. The main rule is to take action without delay and to match one's needs and income. Once it is done all that remains is to file the papers and review the situation annually. If a woman's circumstances change, she can always change things accordingly. At least she can be relatively sure that she will be financially secure on her own, if need be.

Note
It should be emphasized to the reader that the information and advice given in this chapter relates only to the law of England and Wales and no liability shall attach either to the contributors to this chapter or to the authors or to the publisher. Readers are advised in all cases to seek independent legal and financial advice.

9 The Options

Now and again you find yourself thinking about your relationship and your life's direction, and wondering whether you are doing the right thing. You have probably thought about leaving your lover or issuing an ultimatum; you might have considered dating other men; but so far, you have stayed. You might feel lonely and insecure or you may be relatively happy with the status quo, but where is it all leading?

In order to make sense of the future you will have to evaluate the present. You need to look at the strength and potential of the relationship from your personal standpoint. You can then assess where your current course is taking you, and whether this is what you really want.

This chapter helps the mistress, reluctant or wanton, to make her choices. It contains two questionnaires and a summary matrix that looks at her overall position. Chapters 10, 11 and 12 go on to discuss the different options in detail.

Many of us live our lives haphazardly - as events unfold we deal with them. Most of us plan for the future in terms of employment, children's education and pensions, but how many of us take stock of our lives or our relationships to make sure that our life is heading in the right direction? From time to time we ask what is the purpose of life and try to make sense of the future, but events often take over before we have time to act on our thoughts. Consciously or not, we make choices throughout our lives and they shape us and make us what we are.

The mistress is in the unenviable position of total uncertainty as far as her future goes. She might meet somebody else, she might marry her lover or she might end up alone. She feels she cannot plan for anything. The relationship finds it own equilibrium, a routine is established and it is very easy just to let life drift on. She ploughs on with her career, her chances of changing direction growing slimmer as she gets older.

The problem is that she is forever hoping that her relationship will change and she is therefore not making any contingency plans. Ten or fifteen years down the line she might find herself a lonely woman with little security, pension or companionship. She might have given him the best years of her life, but where is she now? The lover has his life established and when he retires chances are that he will not be able to maintain the status quo, even if he wants to. The mistress can't go back, she has made her choices, but probably didn't envisage a life like this. She might have thought that having half a man was better than having none, but she will not be so sure when faced with the facts.

Lord Tennyson wrote "'Tis better to have loved and lost/Than never to have loved at all' - but one wonders. Piet Hein, a Danish poet and writer, said: 'Remember to love, while you dare, remember to live while you do it'. The Danish philosopher Søren Kierkegaard claimed that 'Life is lived forwards but understood backwards', that is, we can only really make sense of our actions after the event. There are no fast and ready answers to the meaning of life. René Descartes maintained that: 'Man is not a means to an end, he is the end itself,' while Anton Chekhov wrote, 'You ask me what life is. It is like asking what a carrot is. A carrot is a carrot.'

Philosophy aside, the mistress is well advised to assess her life with and without her married lover in order to grasp what her position really is, what her choices are, and how they will define her future. She can then evaluate her options and decide whether or not to change direction in the knowledge that she is at least in control. She needs to consider what she would do if he dies, he leaves her, his wife finds out, he's made redundant or her circumstances change. When she knows where she wants to be, she can plan how to get there.

She has several options open to her. She might accept the status quo and continue going nowhere by choice. Alternatively she might decide that she really wants to end the affair. She might decide it is time to force changes, which may involve issuing an ultimatum or making sure that his wife learns of the affair. All need careful consideration, as with most actions there is no turning back. She has to be sure that whatever route she takes she is prepared for and prepared to accept, the consequences.

To evaluate her situation, the mistress needs to take a step back and have a good look at herself and the lover as a couple, as if looking in from the outside. The purpose of the questionnaire below is to begin to evaluate the depth of the relationship and on whose terms the affair is conducted. She should consider how often they meet, whether she can call him, whether he buys her presents or if they have holidays together. The questions are derived from statistics and our interviews with different types of mistresses. It will help the mistress to see, maybe for the first time, the true nature of her relationship and what it means for her future.

Questionnaire 1: The Strength of the Relationship

1. Does he refer to you as his girlfriend?
a) yes
b) no

2. Does he act as your boyfriend to people who don't know the situation?
a) yes
b) no

3. Does he buy you presents for birthdays and Christmas?
a) yes
b) no

4. Does he answer your telephone?
a) yes
b) no

5. Does he look through your post?
a) yes
b) no

6. Does he have keys to your home?
a) yes
b) no

7. Does he advise you on finance, cars and/or home maintenance?
a) yes
b) no

8. Does he do household chores for you?
a) yes
b) no

9. Can you phone him whenever you want?
a) yes
b) no

10. Can you phone him at work?
a) yes
b) no

11. Do you phone each other regularly?
a) yes
b) no

12. Will he look after you if there's an emergency?
a) yes
b) no
c) don't know

13. How long have you been together?
a) under a year
b) one to five years
c) over five years

14. Does he work in senior/higher management?
a) yes
b) no

15. Do you have holidays together?
a) yes
b) no

16. Do you have good sex?
a) always
b) most of the time
c) it is not important

17. Do you miss him when he's not around?
a) extremely
b) to some extent
c) not at all

18. When did you last talk with him about your relationship?
a) within the last week
b) within the last month
c) a long time ago or never

19. Have you asked him whether he would ever leave his wife?
a) yes
b) no

20. If the answer to 19 is yes, did he say:
a) I don't know
b) I can't
c) I never could

21. When did you last talk about your feelings towards each other?
a) within the last week
b) within the last month
c) never or long time ago

22. Do you love him?
a) yes
b) no
c) I think so

23. Do you believe that he loves you?
a) yes
b) no
c) I think so

24. Does he tell you that he loves you?
a) yes
b) no

25. How often do you see him on average per month?
a) four or more times
b) one to three times
c) often I don't see him for months on end

26. Do you see him mainly during day time or evenings?
a) evenings
b) day time

27. Do you normally spend the night together?
a) yes
b) no

28. What is the longest time you have not seen him?
a) up to four weeks
b) two months
c) more than two months

29. Do you display affection openly in public (away from the area where he lives)?
a) yes
b) no

30. Your friends who have met him
a) say that you seem like a married couple
b) say that they can understand why you are with him
c) can't understand what you see in him

For questions that have only a) and b) options, give yourself two points for every a) answer. For questions that have a), b) and c) options, give yourself two points for every a) answer and one for every b) answer.

50 or more: You are hooked and so is he. It is just possible that you will build a life together.
30-50: You have a strong relationship, but can it change?
10-29: Are you sure you are not just hanging in there?
Less than 10: You don't have a relationship. Drop him now!

The results of the questionnaire should be treated with reservation, although it has proven itself to be a good overall measure of the state of the relationship in tests with mistresses we know. Other issues that should be considered alongside the questionnaire are the lover's family circumstances, such as if he has young children or whether his wife does not work (both of these are likely to reduce the overall score). Statistics tell us that the married lover is less likely to leave his marriage in such circumstances.

The next step is to assess and understand how the mistress feels about herself, her current situation, her future and whether she is already on her way to changing things. The questionnaire below works on the same principal as the previous one, that is, it will help the mistress to stand outside the frame and analyse her situation dispassionately.

Questionnaire 2: Happiness and the Future

1. Why are you staying in the relationship?
a) it is convenient and I enjoy his company
b) I love him
c) there will never be anybody else for me

2. Do you want to (re) marry / have a (new) permanent relationship in the future?
a) not necessarily
b) yes
c) no

3. Do you want to marry him?
a) no
b) maybe
c) yes

4. Do you believe he will divorce and marry you?
a) no
b) maybe
c) yes

5. Do you want to have children?
a) not necessarily
b) yes

6. Do you feel isolated and/or lonely?
a) never
b) sometimes
c) most of the time

7. Do you feel you are coping?
a) yes
b) I'm relatively OK
c) I am miserable; I can't take this any longer

8. Do you go out with other men (just dating or more)?
a) yes
b) no

9. Have you advertised in the personal columns or joined an introduction agency?
a) yes
b) no

10. Could you cope with living on your own (or staying in your current marriage) potentially for ever?
a) no problem
b) if I had to
c) I dread it

11. Do you feel financially insecure?
a) no
b) yes

12. Do you have a circle of good friends?
a) yes
b) no

13. Are you close to your family?
a) yes
b) no

14. Is a career important to you?
a) yes
b) no

15. How do you spend your free time (when not with your lover)?
a) I have a lot of hobbies and spend time with my friends and/or family
b) I just make the time pass, watch television, do gardening and household chores, etc.
c) restlessly, waiting and hoping for the phone to ring

16. Do you like yourself?
a) yes
b) no

For questions that have only a) and b) options, give yourself two points for every a) answer. For questions that have a), b) and c) options, give yourself two points for every a) answer and one for every b) answer.

25 or more: You are independent and coping well, making a life of your own.
18-25: You are not as strong as you would like, but you are trying your best.
10-17: You are relying on this relationship for your future.
Less than 10: You are very unhappy and have to make some hard decisions.

The mistress may find that her scores from the two questionnaires vary. She might be relying on the relationship for the future when she is really deluding herself, or quite the opposite. In any case she can reflect on this and start to understand the true nature of her relationship. She should also consider other issues like her financial and employment prospects (for future security), her age and fitness (for dating prospects and for having children) and her strength of character.

The married mistress will, in addition, need to consider whether she wants to leave her marriage, her husband and maybe children and what it would mean to her and them. She will have to evaluate her marriage as well as her affair.

The next step is to put together the two scores in the summary results table, which gives the option of four combinations. The first questionnaire concentrates on the strength of the relationship, while the second seeks to discover whether the mistress is happy and how she is coping with the situation. The resulting squares show the general conclusion of the two, giving a good understanding of how she is positioned in the relationship.

Table 9.1 Summary of Questionnaires

Strength of the relationship

High	*Square A (Q1>29,Q2>17)* You are happy with what you have and it is pretty good. Make sure you are not deluding yourself about your future needs.	*Square C (Q1>29,Q2<18)* You have everything to lose, but you cannot continue as you are.
Low	*Square B (Q1<30,Q2>17)* You are happy with what you have. Enjoy it, but make sure it is OK for the future too.	*Square D (Q1<30,Q2<18)* Just drop it. Your relationship is weak and you are very unhappy. You need to change your life.
	High	*Low*

Level of happiness and coping

Key:

Q1	Questionnaire 1 score
Q2	Questionnaire 2 score

Square A in Table 9.1 shows that the relationship is strong, the mistress is relatively happy with her situation and she doesn't feel that her future is threatened. She is probably very independent and able to manage her own affairs. The danger here is that because the relationship is so solid she is not considering her future needs. It is also possible that, whether or not she is aware of it, there is something in this relationship that suits her. Depending on the detailed scores and the weight she wants to put on individual answers, like whether she wants children, she can plan her way forward.

Square B identifies that the relationship is rather weak, but as in square A, the mistress is quite happy with the situation. She is probably a wanton mistress, a strong and independent character and this 'no-strings' type of affair might suit her well. She might regard the relationship as transitory or she might feel this level of involvement is all she wants. She should, however, consider whether it will be satisfactory in the longer term.

Square C is where most reluctant mistresses will find themselves. The relationship is very strong but she is pretty miserable with her situation, even if she is coping satisfactorily. One thing is certain: this is not what she wants for her life in the future. She will therefore have to consider her options to change the status quo, even if she has a lot to lose. She should study her individual answers to the questionnaires to see what really is important to her and to assess whether this relationship is ever likely to provide it.

Square D is also for reluctant mistresses, and is the worst situation imaginable. Not only is the relationship weak but the mistress is unhappy, and depending on the individual scores she may be a real casualty of affairs. She is best advised to face the facts and get out of there quickly. Unless she makes some changes, she is a likely candidate for depression, and nobody deserves this. If she continues on this route, she is prone to become bitter and end up a lonely old woman, with half a life and not even half a man.

The mistress should now consider her priorities. She needs to make the overall decision of how important this relationship is to her versus her own needs. Her conclusion will dictate, or at least affect, how she plans her life from now on. If she decides to stay with the relationship, either because it suits her, or she is sure that it will lead to changes or she cannot do anything else, she should read Chapter 10. Here we discuss positive schemes for trying to make it all worthwhile. If she decides to leave, Chapters 11 and 12 deal with the often painful process of leaving a man you love and surviving. She might also want to consider changing her stance within what is a rather unfulfilling relationship (that is, she might wish to move from square D into the more satisfactory square B). If she wants to jolt the relationship into a resolution, or at least keep her options open, various courses of action are available.

She could just wait and see, and take no action in the relationship, but be proactive about meeting other men. In most cases, this is not easy. For one thing, being in a relationship already sends out the wrong signals to the opposite sex. For another, if the mistress is really in love then she will inevitably try to substitute her lover rather than finding a genuinely new one. She will look at the prospective suitor and think, well, he isn't really like 'Jim': he is dark instead of blond; too fit/not fit enough; his sense of humour is not quite right; and he doesn't like sailing - whatever it is 'Jim' likes. We are creatures of habit, particularly with relationships, and it is difficult to give new things a chance when you are still bound up with the old. The more detached from her relationship she becomes, the better her chances become. She must try to concentrate on feeling good about herself and give herself the best chance.

If she really can't take it any longer, or decides to see where the lover's loyalties and affection really lie, she could issue an ultimatum: 'If you don't leave your wife, then I will go.' This is dangerous as the outcome is highly unpredictable, but in some cases a positive response might be forthcoming. The lover might just have grown complacent and expect her to stay as she is for as long as he wants her. This might mean that he has never really faced the facts or his own feelings, and if he is confronted he might finally decide to bite the bullet. It could work against the mistress, but if it does, he probably wasn't worth it anyway. If he doesn't know by now what he wants, and/or he can't put his desires into practice, he never will. The mistress should obviously not opt for this high-risk strategy if she is not prepared to lose him, for in most cases, that is exactly what will happen.

If he promises to leave his wife, there is still no guarantee that he will actually do it. Promises are often made in the heat of the moment, and when the lover has time to reflect he might find that either he doesn't want to or can't. He might say, on reflection, that the children are too young, or doing their A-levels, that his wife couldn't take it just now, or that he wouldn't want to upset his parents. All these reasons and more may be genuine enough and, after all, the dilemma is agonizing. The lover might truly love his mistress but still be unable to change his life for her. One could then argue that he does not love her enough, but how do you weigh the value of accepting responsibility for marriage vows and children against loving somebody else? Of course, he should have thought of that before.

He could say yes and appear on the doorstep with suitcases, which is every reluctant mistress's secret dream. This may be the start of a beautiful future but it might also go horribly wrong. Apart from the fact that this is a new and untested arrangement for both of them, the fact is that the lover is likely to go back to his family. He will have to change a lifetime of habits, environment and friends he has come to rely on, and if there are children involved, his guilt may force him back. Between 75 and 85 per cent of men who have affairs are likely to remain with their wives even if they have moved out for a while.[1] The only advice we can give here is that the mistress should keep an open mind, live as she normally does and see what happens. If he goes back, throwing tantrums or crying rarely works and she will have to accept defeat. She will at least know for sure where she stands.

The mistress also has to bear in mind that the lover might separate from his wife and divorce, either at her instigation or his own, or maybe because his wife finds out about his affair. The mistress might expect him to marry her but, according to statistics, only a fraction do.[2] Sometimes the affair has served as a catalyst to bring about the divorce, but often the mistress remains on the sidelines and the man, if he remarries, finds somebody else. This can be tough if the mistress is very dependent on the relationship. Therefore, working at becoming her own woman and happy within herself is a goal that every mistress should aspire to when she plans her future.

More desperate measures are available, such as making sure that the wife does find out, either by writing to her, calling her or even visiting his house in the guise of a market researcher or the like. This is not recommended. The temptation can be great, especially for those who find themselves in squares C and D, but these actions rarely end in a positive outcome for the mistress and only hurt all parties involved.

When the mistress has decided what her options are and how she will act, she will be in a position to plan for other aspects of her life, such as career, employment and financial matters. We would recommend that she plan her life as if she were going to remain single, especially on the financial side. She will probably need additional pension arrangements, health insurance and cover for critical illness and accidents, and general income protection in case of unemployment. If she is financially supported by the lover, which is rare nowadays, she also has to plan for not relying on that income in the event that he ceases to pay. Anything could happen, from the lover deciding to stop his support to his death. In the latter case she would not be entitled to any support unless he has made provision for her in his will. If the mistress decides to continue with the relationship permanently, she should probably discuss this with the lover.

Whatever her situation the mistress should not sit back and wait for things to change. She should take control of her life, decide what is the best strategy for her and act accordingly. This will not be easy, as it means facing facts about herself and her situation that can be painful; but the rewards are potentially great. She will no longer feel without direction, without meaning or hope in life; she will be her own master and survive, whatever happens.

10 Staying in the Relationship

If you are considering staying in your relationship hoping that your lover will eventually leave his wife for you, but suspecting that he will not, this chapter is for you. You are looking, perhaps for the first time, at the possibility of sustaining indefinitely the relationship in its current form despite the fact that you might never marry him. If stay you must, for whatever reason, a number of things must change if you are to survive the potentially painful rollercoaster you are choosing to ride.

There is a wonderful saying that speaks of having the serenity to accept what cannot be changed, the courage to change what can be changed and the wisdom to know the difference. Significantly, it has been employed by numerous organizations that help people to manage addictions, including Alcoholics Anonymous and Narcotics Anonymous. As you read through this chapter, bear in mind the three ingredients – serenity, courage and wisdom – essential for protecting yourself as you embark upon one of the most emotionally turbulent ways of life you could ever choose.

No woman should ever begin a relationship with a married man, let alone remain in it. Not because it is considered morally wrong by most societies in the world, but because it has the potential to do tremendous damage to herself, her lover and his wife and family. While the affair continues, all the people involved, whether directly or indirectly, are at risk. The most obvious potential victims are the lover's wife and family and hence his marriage. The less obvious victim is the mistress herself and although steps will be taken by both parties to the affair to safeguard the marriage, little is done to protect her. Society says that she deserves no protection, that she knows what she is doing and must accept the consequences. To an extent this is perfectly true, yet her major mistake was simply falling in love with the wrong man.

Before we examine the steps a mistress can take to minimize the

adverse affects of the affair on her, we need to address the many
aspects she can do little or nothing about. She must stop dreaming,
start to face reality and accept a number of painful home-truths. If she
finds this all too difficult, she will need to consider whether she should
be staying in the relationship at all.

Given the lack of general approval, the mistress must develop
mental and emotional strength. She does this by learning to believe in
herself and her judgement, and by developing the barriers necessary to
defend herself against condemnation. If she cannot, she will not be
able to tolerate the situation for long. She must find a way of explaining why she is a mistress since people are going to question her
motives. 'Because I love him', as powerful as that statement seems to
her, will never be enough. She will need to confront her attitude to her
lover's wife and children and ask herself a number of uncomfortable
questions. People will, almost without exception, challenge her about
the affair and seldom pleasantly. How does she feel about trying to
'steal' another woman's husband or trying to 'take' a child's father?
Why does she put up with the way her lover treats her? Where is her
self-respect? She must find answers to justify her position to others
and, perhaps more importantly, to herself. If she cannot do this her
shame will help to isolate her.

Each mistress knows that the most significant influence on her is
her lover's marriage. Almost everything that happens will be governed
by the extent to which he feels he has to shield his wife from the affair
and how much he assumes his particular marriage will tolerate. He
will minimize the risks to his home life by restricting the scope of the
relationship with his mistress. Inevitably, she becomes complicit in the
protection of his marriage without even considering it. In this way,
ironically, she helps to preserve the very thing that stands between her
and what she wants. She must appreciate that some marriages are actually strengthened by an affair. Her presence might enable her lover to
stay within an unsatisfactory union with his wife and, rather than
being a threat, the mistress actually becomes an asset. Although few
people would see it that way, the mistress must consider this view seriously, and think about her role within this context. While she is waiting for the marriage to weaken, she is building fragile hopes that will
usually end in disappointment. It is far better that she tries to convince
herself that he is *never* going to leave his wife. If she stays with him
knowing this, she will have to develop the necessary strength or the
relationship will slowly destroy her.

Despite all the evidence to the contrary, the mistress will never
completely lose the dream that one day her lover will want to be with

her forever. This will continue to plague her throughout the affair and she must be prepared to stifle it as best she can. In fact, the minute she truly loses that hope, the relationship will start to end.

She must accept that the longer the affair continues, the less likely her lover is to leave home. Once the first year is over, if nothing has happened, the odds against her rise exponentially. In part this has to do with the establishment of his routine and the place he has found for his mistress in his life, but mostly it is to do with the fact that he begins to view his mistress as a very close friend – albeit a close friend he sleeps with from time to time. As with any confidante, he feels free to discuss most aspects of his life with her which, unfortunately, will include his wife, his children and his life with them. His mistress supports and cares for him, yet he does not have to be with her all the time. He would no more think of leaving his wife for his mistress than he would think of leaving his wife for any other friend – in both cases the roles are completely different and separate in his mind. The mistress needs to understand this differentiation; it is crucial if she is to come to terms with her place in his life.

Ultimately, there are only three basic circumstances in which a mistress stays in such an unsatisfactory relationship. The first is that she is genuinely in love and wants no one else, the second is that she is in love and does not believe she could find someone else anyway, and the third is simply that he is better than nothing. The first is going to be emotionally punishing. The second often becomes a self-fulfilling prophecy but it is more hopeful since it indicates at least the possibility of escape. A relationship based on the third scenario is the easiest to manage but the most likely to wane, since without love she is unlikely to tolerate the situation. Most reluctant mistresses, sadly, fall into one of the first two categories.

We have not yet really focused on the lover in this chapter. It would be wrong to imply that he does not have any say in whether the relationship continues or not but, once the relationship is established, such decisions are normally taken by the woman. The lover is unlikely to understand the magnitude of the compromises being made when his mistress tries to accept the status quo. This, like many other decisions, she will make on her own, and any woman needing her partner's emotional and mental support will find being a mistress increasingly difficult.

Unless he is highly insensitive, which some lovers are, he will know how much his mistress cares for him and that she wants him to leave his wife. That she still remains, when he expects her to leave, first amazes him and then delights him when he realizes that he can, as it were, have his cake and eat it. A few mistresses we interviewed believed that the kindest thing he could do if he has no intention of leaving home, would be to leave his mistress; but most men do not take this step – and most mistresses do not want them to. The fact that he does not leave her initially helps to foster her hopes for the future, but eventually she will realize the truth.

The relationship will develop and will operate in parallel with his marriage but with a number of significant differences that she must learn to accept. She will never have the support afforded to his wife and all that this entails. The impact of this ranges from the simple benefit of having someone else in the home to share the household responsibilities to the more significant aspect of providing for the future. The mistress is extremely unlikely to benefit from her lover's insurance policies, pension and salary and must therefore ensure that she takes steps to guarantee her own financial security.

As long as she stays with her lover, she is normally denying herself the possibility of meeting and perhaps marrying someone else. She may also be forfeiting the opportunity to bear children. She will grow older and what seems bearable at thirty, can assume tragic proportions at fifty when she finds herself on her own, childless and without funds. She occupies such a small place in her lover's life while her lover plays such a large part in hers; in truth the balance in the relationship is overwhelmingly weighted against her. She is in the unique position of being committed to her lover yet having to sustain herself as a single person for as long as the relationship continues in its present form. It is easy for her to lose sight of the fact that she must plan for her future alone rather than assume her lover will always be there. The likelihood is that he will not.

Thinking ahead, even if the relationship with his mistress continues, the lover will be planning for his retirement with his wife, not with his mistress. Any single person has to think ahead, but sometimes it is easy for the mistress to forget that she too, in the end, is on her own. Her ultimate future must be mapped out without him in mind – this is, after all, what he is probably doing to her.

Another issue that the mistress will continue to face is the lack of social acceptance and the condemnation from other people. She does not want to feel ashamed of her relationship but most people will expect her to be. She does not want to hide from society and she will often crave acknowledgement in some form or another. Sadly, it is a forlorn hope.

The lover's wife has a title and a role to play which is recognized, both socially and legally, as valid and legitimate. She can accompany him to business events, call him overtly at the office, walk down the street holding his hand and meet all his friends and family. He can discuss her, her achievements and activities openly with anyone and no one will raise an eyebrow if his sentences begin with 'My wife . . .'. Imagine the response if the word 'mistress' or 'girlfriend' were substituted. The lover's relationship with his wife is reinforced and endorsed by the many opportunities for expression and confirmation; his relationship with his mistress by contrast, is limited by its very unacceptability. There will be many times when this will cause her a great deal of pain. However, the mistress needs to accept she will always be part of her lover's private life, his wife a part of his public life. This will not change.

The mistress must also prepare herself for adverse reactions. She is likely to encounter those who realize or begin to suspect the nature of the relationship. People can be very cruel and feel completely justified in condemning her, whereas the lover is less likely to face the same kind of criticism. Interestingly it is women rather than men who will attack her most vehemently. Perhaps she represents a threat to them, perhaps they relish taking the moral high-ground, or perhaps some feel slightly jealous. The man escapes much more easily. Even today, many believe that men are, by nature, polygamous and therefore prone to adultery whereas women's sexual needs are considered to be more limited. The responsibility is in this way placed wholly on the women. The feminist movement has had some effect on the way in which the sexes interact, but it has not wiped out the general, fundamental belief that it is easier for a woman to control herself when faced with temptation than it is for a man. Conveniently, this is one of the very few areas where women are seen as being stronger than men. What a shame that this rule of thumb is not applied within the working structures of our major companies!

Men are slightly more condemning of the lover than women, but nevertheless most harbour a secret envy of his audacity and his opportunity to bed two women. By contrast, the mistress might have to face the fact that she is often seen as a woman of low morals. She, much more than the lover, will be the subject of malicious gossip, smutty comments and, sometimes, overt and unbridled animosity. It is virtually impossible for her to defend herself in these situations unless she has thought through her motives clearly. She might be prepared to deny the relationship or else admit her involvement openly. The former means that she must lie about something she does not want to lie about and the latter might put her lover at risk. Almost always, the lover's protection is of great concern to her but he will seldom feel the same way about her. Not because he does not care, but simply because he seldom realizes that she is subject to such pressures and she is unlikely to tell him. Some believe that if he knows about the criticism and suspicion he might get nervous and end the affair, and others just see no point in discussing the obvious.

To an outsider, the mistress may appear to be a masochist, succumbing to the pain and insecurity time and time again. Even the most level-headed of them are often idealists who believe totally in love and accept all that love demands of them. This may make them fools in some people's eyes, but it does not make them masochists.

Many also say that the passion of a marital affair is fuelled and sustained only by its very illicitness. They will say that the fact that a mistress cannot have her lover permanently is what keeps her interest. Even some lovers believe this to be so, but in the vast majority of cases it is not true. This is the sort of simplistic observation that only someone who has never been in this situation could make. Except in one's youth, longing based solely on a craving for the unattainable eventually becomes boring. As people mature, the 'treat them mean and keep them keen' mentality earns the contempt it deserves. To suggest that all mistresses are driven solely by the appeal of the unattainable is an insult to both their intelligence and the depth of their feelings.

Those who intimate that a mistress wants only the excitement and would become bored with the mundanities of a normal relationship, like washing, cooking and watching the television, also fail utterly to understand the situation. Doubtless there are a few immature mistresses who crave nothing but adventure, but most long for the normality of day-to-day living. They yearn, for example, to go shopping together in Sainsburys or to choose the colour scheme for the lounge with their lovers – in fact all the aspects that help to anchor a relationship in reality.

The strain of maintaining a part-time relationship, never truly being able to relax, always trying to be on your best behaviour, is immeasurable. People who see only the pleasure and presume that the mistress is deliberately rejecting the rest are missing the point. Each meeting operates under considerable constraints and the lovers try to make best use of their short time together. They are living on borrowed time. It is akin to being given ten minutes to sell yourself at an interview when you know it would take an hour to do it justice. The less time is available, the less able the parties involved are to be themselves. This is not exciting, but exhausting.

As we have said before, the mistress does not want this kind of life. It is clandestine, always under threat, unsupportive and emotionally punishing. She wants a normal relationship with natural conclusions which includes spending most of her time with the man she cares about, participating in a love that evolves and matures, and being affirmed by society, family and friends. In short, she believes she wants to be his wife. Having said this, few mistresses really consider in detail what it would be like to be married to their lovers. They avoid thinking about it too much because they have to convince themselves repeatedly that it will never happen.

When interviewing mistresses, we pursued this particular point doggedly. We asked what they suspected it might be like and investigated how they would feel about marrying someone who, as they well knew, was an adulterer. Their reaction was eye-opening. Though some admitted that they could probably forgive a one-night stand, none believed that she could accept it if her lover, having become her husband, had a long-standing affair. It was not the sexual infidelity that concerned them so much as the personal intimacy of the extra-marital relationship. On first sight, this appears contradictory. After all, this is exactly what the mistress is providing for her lover. She can accept that her lover is unfaithful to his wife, but would not accept it if the tables were turned. She also accepts that her lover probably still has sex with his wife. So while he is her lover his infidelity is accepted, yet if he were to become her husband it suddenly becomes unacceptable.

This response seems hypocritical but the reasoning is simple. The mistress knows that her lover's wife was there first and also considers that she has the right, as part of the marriage contract, to make certain demands of her husband. In particular, she has the right to protest about his infidelity. The mistress does not believe that her own situation warrants equivalent status. She would never, for example, ask him to stop having sex with his wife, no matter how much she might want to. She considers herself to be an interloper and does not accord herself equal rights if, indeed, she accords herself any rights at all. The very fact of her existence tells her something about the nature of his relationship with his current wife – a relationship that the mistress would never want with her husband.

Extramarital relationships operate in extraordinary circumstances – some pleasurable, some not. Despite these pressures, or perhaps because of them, the two people involved form an unusual bond based predominantly on the way they interact and very little else. They are not held together by marriage, history, family life or by numerous shared moments – all that holds them together is their feelings for each other. For those relationships that endure, these feelings supersede lust and develop to include friendship, trust, affection, care and love; they might even thrive as a result of the couple's relative independence. Like the orchid, the intensity and depth of some relationships can flourish only in very specific conditions. Certainly, it appears that both participants tend to find their passion sustained for much longer than in ordinary relationships.

We asked mistresses which they would prefer – to sustain the magic of the relationship but forgo marriage, or marry and then find out that the magic had evaporated. Their answers were unanimous. Many people would argue that the demise of passion is exactly what would happen if the lover ever married his mistress; that this marriage would eventually settle into – at best – one part excitement to four parts routine. They would also suggest that whatever caused him to stray in the first place might ultimately reappear in the new partnership. This may or may not be true, but for the individuals concerned it has to be an article of faith – nothing can be proven one way or another until after the event.

The mistresses we spoke to believed that the depth of feeling could be sustained if they married their lovers. Unfortunately, most of their partners thought it would die. Statistics tend to support the lovers given that second and subsequent marriages are more likely to end in divorce than first marriages. However, so few men actually marry their former mistresses that these statistics might not apply – not enough people have tested out the theory. In any case statistics do little to deter the dreams and beliefs of people in love.

The mistress might not have legal rights but she certainly has basic human rights and, whether the lover likes it or not, he should be persuaded to take some responsibility for her well-being. The lover presumes that the mistress accepts his marital relationship and the fact that he is responsible for his wife and family but not for her; it is easy for her not to question the validity of his assumption.

People in Western societies are uncomfortable about the concept of polygamy, yet in such arrangements all the husband's wives are acknowledged and maintained. Those who consider these marriages to exploit women would do well to consider the alternative of the monogamous society that tacitly recognizes the fact that a man may take a mistress but, at the same time, does not insist that she is cared for.

The mistress must not allow her lover to shirk all responsibility for her. This does not necessarily mean that he should sustain her financially, but it does mean that he should not be allowed to treat her badly. She knows that he has much to lose – his wife, his children, the respect of his peers and friends, his money and his home. She continues to make excuses for him, trying well beyond the realms of reason to understand his behaviour and convince herself that he wants to be with her but simply cannot. The harsh reality is summed up by the phrase, 'Those that want to, find a way; those that don't, find excuses'. He remains with his wife because this is what he wants most. If he cancels a meeting with his mistress it is because whatever else he is doing matters more. A painful question the mistress could ask is 'If I were a million pounds, would he still cancel?' The answer is probably no. However, it is not true that she has to put up with the unpredictability, inconvenience and frustration. What she must try to do is establish ground rules that dictate some of the parameters within which the relationship will operate. This is often a difficult subject for the mistress to tackle since her inclination is to be acquiescent to the complexities of her lover's life, but, within reason, there are a number of changes she can and should make.

First, she must establish some form of access to her lover so that she can contact him if necessary. Calling him at home is unlikely to be acceptable, and rightly so, but phoning the office, sending him letters or communicating using a friendly third party are all options. The simple act of establishing her right to access, even limited access, accords the mistress with some element of control, so that she is not subject continually to the lover's desire as to when and if to initiate contact.

Next she must ensure, to the best of her ability, that her lover is aware of her feelings, needs and insecurities. So many mistresses hide their confusion and pain from their lovers, always trying to avoid being a problem or appearing too dependent on him. This is a mistake. The lover has chosen to enter into and sustain this relationship – it is not a cross that the mistress must bear alone, but their joint responsibility. She does not have to be a doormat. He is not going to leave her simply because she is being difficult or less than excellent company; nor is her compliance going to make him love her more. If he cares for her, he will want to know how she is feeling, and if he does not, she has little to lose by being herself.

Mostly, she does not feel loved even if her lover tells her so repeatedly. She has difficulty absorbing the contradiction of a man who says he loves her yet never appears to put her first. All she knows is that he is not with her and this leads her to doubt the sincerity of her lover's affections. Trying to sustain his interest by pretending to be something she is not is both dishonest and unnecessary. By showing some of her frailties, she may be surprised by his reaction. If she pretends that she is strong, happy and coping well, it is hardly surprising that her lover presumes that the relationship meets her requirements. He is never going to know how she feels or what she wants if she does not tell him.

The relationship will never be fair on her and she will seldom come first in her lover's life. Although she knows that he is married, this does not mean that her needs are not important – they are. She must believe that, on occasions, she has a right to feel cheated, frustrated and angry and not be persuaded by her lover that she is being unreasonable.

One of the subjects that most mistresses find difficult to talk about is children. Yet if the relationship continues for a number of years, the subject is bound to arise, if only in her mind. She might be tempted to get pregnant without consulting her lover, either because she desperately wants children or in an attempt to force the lover to leave his wife. This is misguided, an abuse of both the lover and the unborn child, rather than an act of love. If the mistress wants her lover's baby, she should find the courage to discuss it openly with him. His reaction might not be what she would like to hear, but at least it will tell her a great deal about the nature of the relationship. If children are important to her, but her lover does not want them with her, then she has a major decision to make – her lover or children. The mistress must remember that this is one of the few events in her life that is limited by time. If, without previous consultation, he is suddenly faced with her pregnancy, he could react in a number of ways. He might leave her immediately, fearing that the child will force the affair into the open. He might refuse to support the child after it is born. He might actually leave his wife, but the mistress will never know whether he left for her or the baby. If he leaves home because he feels forced into action, it is possible that he might resent both his mistress and his child later in the relationship. He may be overjoyed and take responsibility for the child, but still stay with his wife. In most cases the child will be denied the permanent presence of a father and might lose him altogether. He might, of course, marry his mistress and they might live as a happy family from then on, but, to be frank, this is the least common outcome.

Another temptation for even the kindest mistress is the occasional overwhelming desire to tell his wife about the affair. The motivation for this could be pure frustration with the impasse, a wish to lash out when in pain, resentment that his wife has everything she (the mistress) wants, or simply to try to force her lover's hand. Again this would be more akin to vengeance than love, and fortunately very few mistresses let themselves be guided by such impulses. Besides, even if disclosure was to destroy the lover's marriage, it is extremely unlikely that he would turn to his mistress afterwards. He is most likely to be furious and the mistress risks losing his love and respect forever. Perhaps his wife does have a right to know, but it is not the mistress's place to take responsibility for the revelation. In most cases, his wife has done nothing wrong and hurting her so deliberately is callous and unnecessary.

Resentment of the lover's wife is common and it is easy for the mistress to cast her as the villain. But often nothing is further from the truth. The wife, however, does have the one thing that the mistress craves more than anything else: time. Time rules the relationship and governs what is and what is not possible. The mistress will do everything within her power to maximize every available moment often to her detriment. She naturally wants to spend as much time as possible with her lover, but the unpredictability of their meetings usually plays havoc with her life. She might have to respond to his invitations at a moment's notice or wait for days, and sometimes weeks, between telephone calls. If she is not careful, she will fall into the trap of postponing all aspects of her life just in case her lover might call. Although such behaviour is regrettably common, it is a way of life that will damage her in two significant ways. First, her life will diminish as she denies herself many of the other opportunities on offer and second, she will look to her lover to provide all the interest in her life thereby increasing the pressure on the relationship and magnifying his importance in her eyes.

If we accept that she cannot change the way she feels about her lover and that she does not want to remove him from her life, then she must take steps at least to move him from the centre to the sidelines. In short, she must strive to place him where he has placed her. She does this not by diminishing what she feels for him but by increasing everything else. This takes careful planning and a dogged determination to succeed. Ideally the mistress should try to prearrange meetings with her lover so that she can plan the rest of her time fruitfully. But, as any mistress will tell you, this is not always possible. Her alternative is to plan her life anyway and resolve, to the best of her ability, not to cancel arrangements with other people or for other events.

The people who bear the brunt of her unpredictability are her friends and she must take great care not to abuse their goodwill. The mistress will need her friends; they were there before the lover appeared on the scene and will be around long after he has gone. She will need their understanding, support and reassurance when the going gets tough – as it most certainly will. To treat them continually as if they were less important than the lover is to risk losing them alto-gether. They might understand being put off if something wonderful happens, like the lover turning up with two aeroplane tickets, but they will not tolerate being treated as second-class citizens forever. The other common mistake that many mistresses make, by contrast, is to overburden their friends with the pain and woe of their situations. Even the closest of confidantes eventually become bored with the tales of neglect, especially if they believe that the mistress should leave her lover anyway. It is hard for them to watch someone they care about banging their head against a brick wall and then telling everyone how much it hurts; their patience will eventually evaporate taking them with it. The mistress has chosen her situation, and the pain, like the pleasure, simply goes with the territory.

As soon as possible, she should start to plan her life without her lover in mind. There are places to go and people to see; holidays to take and things to learn. She should look ahead, perhaps as much as ten years, and try to visualize what her life will be like then. In partic-ular she should consider what would be left after taking her lover out of the equation. Then she must plan what she wants to achieve and how to reach her goal. This may be frightening because the future often appears to be a black hole. However, this exercise will serve to focus her mind and show her that she must take charge of her life immediately if she is to grow as a human being and not be constrained by the limitations of her current relationship. Above all, she must resist the temptation to become a victim, with no control over her situation.

Although it is unlikely that she will want another relationship, this does not preclude her seeking the close friendship of other men. If she is single, she is a free agent and should behave like a single woman. This includes dating. Even if she decides to be faithful to her lover, male friends could accompany her to dinner parties or events at work, and, if appropriate, could provide her with a male perspective on her situation. To avoid other men completely denies her the opportunity, albeit small in her mind's eye, to meet someone with whom she might be able to conduct a normal relationship and who might offer the possibility of life beyond her affair.

It is difficult being a mistress. It is difficult to love a man who belongs to someone else, to want someone so much that you are prepared to put up with the stress, the condemnation and the uncer-tainty that the relationship presents day after day. It is difficult know-ing that the very fact of your existence is probably helping to preserve your lover's marriage, or at least making it more bearable, in one way or another. It is difficult knowing that the odds are stacked overwhelmingly in your rival's favour. The mistress's greatest enemy is always herself, yet although she might have to accept many constraints, she can make a number of significant changes to her life that might make the affair a little easier to manage. Perhaps the reluctant mistress should learn some lessons from the wanton mistress and position her lover in his rightful place – in a corner of her life, albeit a special and wonderful corner. She cannot change him; she can only change herself; and although she cannot stop loving him, if she wants to stay, she must learn to diminish his effect on her. We hope that with luck, and with perseverance, she either learns to survive or finds a way out.

11   Ending the Relationship

You may have come to the decision that you must end this relationship or it will, slowly but surely, destroy you. You may be so tired of the continuous see-saw of happiness and misery in your life that you suddenly feel you no longer have a choice. You want your life back. You may also have reached the point where your frustration and even anger is such that you feel ready to drop him and start anew.

Leaving the man you love is always painful and heart-breaking, whatever your situation, and your friends cannot understand why this should be so. You know that it is not a simple case of being sensible. You will have to learn to manage your emotions and regain control of your life, before you can succeed in leaving him behind and finding happiness in your life without him.

This chapter gives you a roadmap for how to prepare to leave, giving practical advice on how and when (or if) to end the relationship and how to deal with the immediate aftermath. We also discuss the psychological difference between men's and women's views of their relationships and why your lover prefers to continue living two lives.

One way to understand the mistress's dilemma – should she leave or stay in the relationship? – is to recognize that being a mistress arouses ambivalent emotions which leave her uncertain about what to think, feel or do. She is in love with the lover, he may tell her that he loves her, and yet he still stays with his family. His arguments as to why may sound understandable and even sensible, but they do not help her or alter her situation. Most of us have a view as to what our lives should ideally be and we work towards the goal of giving meaning to our existence. The mistress is no different, but in her case she has an unattainable goal, that of her lover being hers alone. If she fails to make any headway towards this aim, she will in time begin to feel slighted and doubt her own worth. Such doubts are deeply threatening to her personal identity and often lead to overpowering feelings of anger, jealousy, hope and sadness. She still hopes that a positive outcome is possible, but she is beginning to accept that this is unlikely. The more important this goal, the stronger the emotions that ensue. The lover becomes the centre of her world, a reference point that distorts her life; she remains a slave to her love and desperation, thereby thwarting her other life goals and challenging her beliefs.

It would be easy to say, as many people do, that the mistress should just detach herself from her emotions and think sensibly. Her friends are likely to pose the following questions: Does she want to stay a married man's mistress forever? Isn't she worth more? What does she get out of it? Does she really think that he will leave his wife and family for her? The mistress's answers to these questions will usually tally with her friends, (no, yes, not enough, no) and she can see the sense in leaving the lover, but her question is how could she possibly leave somebody she loves. He has become part of her life and the consequences of losing him seem too much to take. Her response is not based on feelings alone, for she has thought about her situation as rationally as possible. The problem is that there are so many potential future scenarios and so many uncertainties. The thoughts that go through her mind encompass a wide range of fears, doubts and hopes: she may be on her own forever and she might not learn to enjoy single life, she might meet and fall in love with somebody else (unmarried) and the lover might finally leave his family for her when he realizes what he is missing.

It is a myth that emotions are irrational and have no relation to thought or reasoning; in fact they are inseparable. We rationalize emotion on the basis of our own experiences, goals and beliefs. We are each, therefore, unique in our approach. There is not one reality but many. Strong feelings are difficult to manage and the reasoning can become clouded because we are unable to make sense of complex facts and feelings. This results in either under- or over-control of emotions. When people refer to thinking with the heart or the head, this is what they mean. It is therefore very tough for the mistress to just be sensible and end the relationship, as she has an uphill struggle to make any logical sense of the way she feels. Reassurance by other people will be little consolation; others will already have told her how she is spoiling her life, how she deserves better and how the lover will never leave his wife. The mistress knows that if she could just leave him (and stop loving him) it would probably be a great relief in the long run. The knowledge, however, is not enough. She needs to learn to manage her emotional state and, in particular her fear of losing love and never finding it again; and she has to develop a sense of certainty in her future well-being.

The mistress's first thoughts about leaving her lover coincide with the natural progression of the relationship. In the beginning she probably dismisses the fact that her lover is married, at first because she probably anticipates a short affair, and later, because she becomes convinced that love will conquer all obstacles. How could he do anything else but leave his wife? He loves her. When this does not happen, and the relationship reaches stalemate, she gets progressively unhappier about the situation and does everything she can to change it. She might write to him or confront him face to face, explaining how difficult the relationship is for her. Often, however, the lover will dismiss these efforts as just the inevitable downside to having a mistress and not really understand (or admit that he understands) the anguish she is experiencing. He might even say, 'You always talk about this every three months or so – I was expecting this,' which somehow makes her feel that she has transgressed or, at least, that to raise it is completely pointless. To have her feelings so disregarded makes her feel inadequate as a person, for her deepest emotions are treated as merely a minor, expected hiatus in the smooth running of the affair. The lover's stance will often make her wonder whether he really loves her and whether she should push for a decision at all. But of course, just when she doubts he loves her, he will say that he does after all, underscoring his declaration with flowers, presents or a lovely dinner. This might increase her hope of a future with him and delay her decision to end the relationship, maybe not for the first time.

Perhaps the starting-point for the mistress on course for leaving her lover is to understand the difference between how men and women think. A man has to be seen to do things right, at least within socially accepted limits. The central theme to a man's thinking is that he has got to be successful. Male success can be defined as having the right building blocks forming the foundation of his life as well as all the appropriate peripherals that show how well he is doing. His foundation consists of career or job, wife, children and extended family. The peripherals are other elements like car, house, financial security, friends and, sometimes, a mistress. The man looks out to the world from his base, the bedrock of his life, without which he would feel unanchored and adrift. Love does not necessarily play an important role in his life; if he has love in his marriage he is grateful, but if not, then he will make the best of it. His marriage represents for him a commitment he has to keep. If he is bored, or in any way dissatisfied with his relationship, he may look for affairs and end up taking a mistress, but he rarely considers leaving his base for her unless the marriage is intolerable or he is, consciously or subconsciously, looking for a way out. He may be genuinely in love with his mistress but he cannot jeopardize his foundation. In his mind he cleaves ruthlessly to the positive sides of his two lives and actively banishes any negative thoughts that sometimes surface, such as his own selfishness or the fact that he is betraying his wife as well as his mistress. When he is with the mistress he lives in a fantasy world, a self-contained bubble, completely detached from everyday life. Despite this, from time to time he might talk to his mistress about his other life, as though refusing to lose himself too much in his alternative life.

A woman thinks and acts differently. Central to her life are love, friendship and sharing a life with a man. Add children and parents, and you have the woman's base. Friends and career are adjuncts, which, while maybe important, rarely take precedence over the base. If a woman is not happy with her relationship, she will do everything she can to repair it, but if she cannot, she will admit it, at least to herself, and consider leaving. This is not to say that she does not regard her responsibilities seriously or honour commitment. Contrary to men, however, a married woman finds it difficult simply to focus on the positive aspects of, say, two relationships; living two lives is nearly impossible, as many of the married mistresses we interviewed testified. If she cannot give love and friendship to her partner, she feels she should not be there. If she loves somebody else, she should be with him. The opinions and pressures of society, family and friends do not normally deter her – it is another matter if she truly cannot do what she wants, because of financial constraints or other pressing family issues. The single mistress lives two lives as well, and her situation may have similarities with the Intermittent Spouse Syndrome, identified as a pattern of symptoms, including anxiety, depression and sexual difficulties, recognized in the wives left at home by spouses who are frequently absent due to work commitments.[1] The underlying cause for these symptoms is the anger felt (but largely unexpressed) at what she experiences as desertion every time her husband leaves home. Maybe the lover balances the desertion of one [woman] with the joining of the other, something the single mistress, at least, cannot do.

Even if the mistress understands this difference of rationalizations, feelings and behaviour between the sexes, it still doesn't change how she views herself, and the inner turmoil she is experiencing continues. His way of dealing with the relationship is too alien to her, and, frankly, understanding how he can continue as usual does not help her a lot. All she wants is a normal life, or, rather, she wants to be the only woman in his life.

At this stage the mistress will start to doubt the very substance of her relationship and to consider leaving it for good. She knows by now that it will take a miracle to change things and that the lover, having alternated between her and his wife for so long, is likely to want to perpetuate the status quo. It might take a long time before she feels ready or frustrated enough to take action; she might shy away from a decision many times (sometimes the lover knows this but says nothing), but in the end she gathers all her strength and determination and takes the plunge.

The lover might meanwhile grow tired of the mistress or fall out of love with her, but that is always possible for either party over time. He might also drop the mistress if her involuntary, intermittent bursts of reasoning – getting him to understand the seriousness of her situation – become too frequent, as this makes him uncomfortable and feel forced to take a stand on his two lives, loves and commitments. He might also decide to leave her if he feels that his wife suspects the affair or if she actually finds out about his philanderings. The man's response is usually to go back to base. He might also find somebody else, another mistress who is easier to control in the short term, as the early stages of an affair are easier for him to handle. Men have a preference for 'crossing the bridge when they come to it', that is, to deal with problems only when they appear.

The doubts about the future of the relationship in the mistress's mind will have to be very strong to enable her to end the relationship. She will have to convince herself that leaving her lover is the best thing she can do for herself, and that she can cope with both doing the deed and its aftermath. The easiest time to leave him would have been in the beginning, when he told her he was married, but it is rare to find a mistress, or indeed anybody, who has the strength of mind required to quit a promising, new love. After that, there might have been a few occasions when she thought about leaving, such as Christmas and holidays. But after enduring those long and painful separations, she has seen her resolutions evaporate on meeting him again.

When the mistress finally decides to make the break she needs to prepare for it well. Doubts will invade her mind, mainly about whether she will cope with the decision and whether her determination will last. She has to plan how she will survive the ensuing heartache, remain absolutely clear about her priorities and not falter from her decision. She should also question her lover to confirm his outlook towards her and to gauge his likely responses to her leaving. Then, it is crucial to decide when and how best to leave. Finally, she has to plan what position she will adopt when faced with his reaction.

At first, the mistress will be assailed by doubts: 'How can I live without him? I will be lonely. I will never meet anybody I can love like him.' It might feel like that to her; in many ways it is like that. The intensity of the relationship means that she experiences loneliness in a more poignant way than she would being on her own or in a normal relationship. Being alone by choice is very different from being lonely because the lover is with his family. Her whole life is governed by his availability; the restricted time they have together means that the relationship remains forever out of kilter. There is never enough time to explore how it would work if they were together as a normal couple; there is only time for enjoyment and best behaviour. In some ways, then, this love is not real.

Most of us want one person to love and share our life with, and the mistress is no exception. Often the significance of this love will for her be heightened by emotions artificially enhanced by the circumstances. She will therefore quite naturally think that she will never meet another she could love as much. She may have kept her options open, dating other men from time to time, but always found disappointment. Ending the relationship and risking being left alone for the rest of her life is therefore a frightening and unwelcome proposition.

The next set of thoughts will centre on the effects that leaving could, with wishful thinking, achieve: 'He can't possibly live without me. Perhaps he will leave his wife if I leave him.' The lover, however, already lives more than half of his life without her. If she leaves, he may be shocked into action, like persuading her to stay or promising to marry her, but most often these acts are just to make her stay within the current arrangement and have no real meaning. Our advice would be never to end the relationship with the hope of forcing his hand.

The mistress's third phase is to weigh up other options which might win her lover, such as telling his wife, or spreading rumours of his affair. As the mistress will in most cases know his address, his home telephone number and other intimate family details, this would not be difficult. There will probably be photographs (taken on a stolen weekend), cards for birthdays, Christmas and the like to prove the affair beyond any reasonable doubt, but in reality very few mistresses take such extreme action. Somehow it contravenes the unwritten agreement between mistress and lover, and of course it rarely benefits the mistress. The lover may be turned out from his home, but he is unlikely to seek solace with his mistress. Our advice is, don't do it! It will only mean heartache for all parties. The only positive thing to emerge is that the mistress will get rid of the lover this way, so it is a kind of last resort.

Last, some will consider secretly shunning contraception and letting nature take its course, especially if the mistress has no children of her own and if she is in her late thirties or early forties. Many will decide against this as morally wrong, some will 'subconsciously' forget to take the odd pill and some might resolve to have his child, if possible. Such an action might be calculated, but it is a natural desire for a woman to want to bear a child to the man she loves, even if she knows that the lover is unlikely to welcome the news. A mistress would rarely resort to conceiving in order to gain the lover, for she knows that she is likely to lose him. One of the mistresses we interviewed said that her lover, when asked what he would do if she became pregnant, said that he would respect her decision (to have the child or not) and would support her financially, if necessary. He neither said nor implied that it would change their relationship in any way.

After this excruciating thought cycle, if the mistress is still determined to end the relationship, she must reassess both her relationship and her life. First and foremost, she has to think long and hard about what leaving him actually means for her future, against what it would mean if she stayed. She needs to understand why she is still with him and how dissatisfied she is with her current life. She needs to ask herself whether she can take the tough reality of not having him around and whether she is ready for the single life that awaits her. At this point, she might have thoughts about her lover being the best there is for her; on the other hand, she might decide to embrace a new freedom of meeting others on her own grounds and terms, something she hasn't been able to do for a long time. All these aspects will differ in importance from mistress to mistress; each individual will have to weigh them personally in order to get a perspective on her life.

Needless to say, her chances of meeting someone new, someone perhaps more exciting, suitable, handsome, sexy, attractive, rich (whatever it is she is looking for or finds attractive) and *not married* are increased if she is single again. However, she must consider how she will react to being available again and maybe finding no takers or at least not the kind she would want. She must also be prepared for the time it will take her to exorcize the lover far enough from her heart and mind; she is unlikely to be ready to fall in love for a long time.

When one is in love it is near impossible to believe that there could ever be anybody else. A number of mistresses we spoke to had tried to find somebody else, some half-heartedly, some with zest, but normally without success. Others would not even contemplate this, feeling fated to endure their lot. The ones who had tried, whether through personal columns or just by going out with friends and being available, often found that they were looking to replace their lover with a very similar substitute. Such women are clearly still in love; their lovers epitomize what they are looking for in a man and nobody else will do. It is hard, if not impossible, to find an identical twin.

In reality most women and men meet somebody else when they have nobody, or at least love nobody, but not before. When this is the case, the subconscious need to replace the lover with somebody similar is absent. Looking back on previous girl/boyfriends illustrates this well, as they are normally very different to each other. Short or tall, witty or serious, there is usually no pattern, just something in the person that excited our interest. The mistress can also consider her past relationships in the light of how she changed through them and how that affected her next relationship. The mistress might genuinely feel that her lover is the only one for her, but she might recall that she once felt that way about a former boyfriend. Love assumes different shapes and any two people interact in a highly particular way, forming a love which is unique. The mistress, if she has decided to end the relationship, can use this argument to strengthen her resolve to change her life and find out what she wants.

The mistress should also think about the positive changes that leaving her lover should bring, and use it to strengthen her determination and belief in her future. Once she is past the pain of leaving and settling to her new life, she will find herself stronger and more able to enjoy life again. The see-saw of happiness and misery has departed, as have her frustration and anger with her lover. She is now liberated to concentrate on her life. She has expended so much energy on mere survival that it may come as a surprise when she finally is free and realizes all the things she has not thought of or acted on during the relationship. This may sound far-fetched to anyone currently a mistress, and we are not saying that the process is easy or that it happens the next day, but she will, eventually, get her life back.

The mistress might find it worthwhile making one last effort to convert her lover or, rather, to harden her resolve. There is nothing quite like hearing and understanding the truth from the source. She does need to be sure that he is determined not to change things, and that the best thing she can do is to leave. We list below the questions that she might ask and the probable answers of a man who will stay in his marriage:

Mistress: What do I mean to you?
Lover: You have a special place in my heart.
          You are exciting.

I love you, really.
I live for the times we meet.

Mistress: Why are you with me?
Lover: You are different, I can talk to you, and you don't have any hang-ups.
          Sex is better with you.
          My wife doesn't understand me.
          My wife has affairs – we have an open marriage.
          I want to be with you.

Mistress: What does your wife mean to you?
Lover: I made a commitment to her.
          We raised the children, she's been . . .
          She is my wife.

Mistress: Why don't you leave your wife?
Lover: I married her and I made a commitment. I can't leave her now.

Mistress: Why are you not with me?
Lover: I can't.
          You would find me boring.
          You deserve better.
          I dream about it.
          You will be OK without me – you don't need me.
          I couldn't divorce because of the children.
          I couldn't divorce because of money.
          I couldn't divorce because of my family.
          It wouldn't work (you would leave).

All of these answers are typical of a man who will not leave his wife. Questioning further his priorities and opinions, the mistress may find that he believes mistresses to be something completely different from wives, a race apart. While obviously untrue, it is convenient for the man to look at things in this way. Lovers hold other characteristic views in common: many women (wives) let themselves go (meaning they are past caring about their appearance); mistresses look better; wives are unadventurous at sex while mistresses are abandoned; wives won't do things with them that mistresses will. All these views are of course stereotypical, but it is surprising how many lovers express them. There are simple explanations for most of these statements, for example a mistress might make more of an effort to 'look better', purely because she sees her lover comparatively rarely. Nobody in a permanent relationship would always go to such trouble, and nor should they.

Asking these questions and getting most of the standard answers will show the mistress that her lover is, in fact, not unique and that he is unlikely to change. He will not leave his wife. She will now have to go for it. The next thing to plan is when and how, and prepare for the aftermath.

To end the relationship successfully, the mistress needs to be in the best or the worst frame of mind for leaving for good. It is a contradiction, but extreme circumstances make it easier to drum up the determination required. Ideally, she should not leave him when she feels low, too emotional, angry, alone or just plain hopeless; she should choose a time when she is strong and has other things to occupy her mind. If she cannot do that she should not despair; determination and timing are all that matters. The mistress should opt for a time when she can be with friends, or before she goes on holiday, or when she is busy with either her family or her work. The more distractions from her normal routine she can plan the better. For some, it may be the perfect time to place that contact advertisement in the paper or resurrect a couple of old acquaintances. Even if they come to nothing, they will bring some variety to life. They could make life fun again! Having somebody to stay is another good strategy. All these measures simply change her routine and leave the mistress much less alone with her thoughts. It may be an idea to encourage thoughts that the lover never really cared because he preferred his wife. After all, if he really had loved her he would be with her now. As he is not, his motives were probably excitement, boredom, fantasy, escape, sex, status or a combination of these. Perhaps he was just weak.

Humour is in short supply at this stage, but it is worth taking a hard look at this man. He's a bit pathetic really. He says he loves the mistress, but that he can't (won't) leave his wife and he will see her only when his work appointments allow. Often he will expect the mistress to be faithful to him, even though he has two women. He will play the family man to his colleagues, friends and neighbours and in some cases expect to be accepted by the mistress's friends and play 'couples' with her quite happily. He is a hypocrite. Who is this man? Why on earth does the mistress take him so seriously? Perhaps she should give him a taste of his own medicine, before she leaves him, and refuse always to be available when he wants her. Laughing at him when he complains that he can only make that one day in the near future is refreshing. She may soon find that whereas she cannot affect the lover's position, she can change her own attitude. She can then tell him all about the other, exciting strings to her bow (make them up if need be!), bringing equality into the relationship at long last. If the mistress succeeds, it will be easier for her to find that right moment to send this man away.

In ending the relationship, the mistress will have to consider what she is able to do and how she will respond to the situation. If she tells him face to face, it will be difficult to even start the leaving conversation as he might arrive with a smile on his face, tell her how much he has missed her, kiss her and maybe even carry her straight to the bedroom. She needs to be extremely focused to handle this, as she will want to relax her determination and promise herself to do it next time. Writing a letter will make sure that she achieves her objective, but it is difficult to say everything that needs to be said and the mistress will never quite know how the lover reacted. He might call her to discuss it or he may accept it and make no contact. The latter will make the mistress feel that the relationship is unresolved, and she will be tempted to call him. This in turn might start the relationship anew. Ending the relationship on the telephone requires a lot of nerve; it is quick but not necessarily any better. As with the letter, the mistress will not know the lover's real response and the likelihood for subsequent phone calls is high unless she has carefully prepared what she will say and is determined not to take his calls. Again, it is likely that the relationship will feel unfinished, making the aftermath worse.

One of the mistress's more successful formulas is to make it impossible to restart the relationship unless the circumstances are changed, for example unless the lover leaves his wife to join the mistress. The objective is to make the lover finally understand and accept how damaging the relationship is, and has been, for her, how she cannot continue destroying herself, how she loves him but knows that he will never leave his wife and how she has to leave him for the sake of her own life. She should tell him how she feels unrespected, how her self-confidence is constantly undermined, what it means to live on the borders of his life and have no control or say in the relationship. She should tell him about all the letters she has written and never sent, the times of despair and happiness – and her determination and absolute need to end it now.

She might have tried some of the above before, but the difference is that she should lay all her cards on the table. This is not easy, as she will feel exposed and vulnerable. She should not be bitter, she should not question his (or her own) love and she must be strong in her conviction to leave. She should not mention his wife or children, nor descend to sarcasm, nor devalue the relationship, nor issue any ultimatums, nor ask him to leave his wife – but just say that she cannot continue. Very few men will be able to avoid discussing the relationship seriously, even if they usually do. If he loves her, he will find it difficult not to feel guilty or accept his selfishness and hypocrisy, and he will let her go.

If she is successful, the relationship will evolve to a deeper level and never be the same again, for a new honesty will have grown between them. Parting in this way is more positive for the mistress, as she will regain some of her self-respect. She might find that her doubts about whether he really loves her are dispelled and she will have more strength to cope with her decision. They have a good chance of remaining friends; the lover might well support the mistress in her decision and come to her aid, if necessary. The downside is that she might find it more difficult to build her new life without him, as they will remain in contact. There is a real danger of feeling that matters have gone from bad to worse, as her emotional tie to the lover is still strong and she sees less of him than ever before. This option is therefore not for the faint-hearted. In any event, it is unlikely for the relationship to be resumed, unless the lover cannot cope with his situation and decides to leave his marriage.

In order to achieve the above, the mistress will probably need to meet and talk to the lover more than once about her wish to end the relationship. She might also want to write to him to explain her feelings in a way he cannot dismiss, and then talk to him again. This is a lengthy process, but it ensures that the lover understands her situation and that the relationship, as it was, comes to a firm end.

Whichever way the mistress ends the relationship she must prepare for his reaction. She should be aware that if she chooses a face-to-face meeting or a telephone call, she opens a two-way conversation. Her lover is likely to either ask her what it is she wants and how things could be changed (to make her stay), or he might be resigned to her right to have a normal life. In the first scenario, the lover might promise the earth just to make her change her mind – after all, she is a woman and will no doubt calm down later. These promises are seldom kept, and soon the relationship will revert to its former state. All the effort the mistress put into ending the relationship has then gone to waste and she will be an emotional wreck. In case the lover says that he will leave his wife for her, the mistress will have to have planned her response in advance. To make her position absolutely clear, she should refrain from seeing him until he has told his wife and actually separated. Otherwise, it might never happen. She must also consider the fact that most men who leave their wives and family under these circumstances eventually go back.

The second scenario is probably more common. If the lover is genuinely in love with the mistress, he will have developed a sense of responsibility towards her as he has for others who form an integral part of his life. Acutely aware of the unfairness of her situation, he will still normally put these considerations aside and live for the moment. The mistress will often aid and abet him in doing just that, as she is delirious with joy to see him and they have great times together. When the man in love is faced by his mistress ending the relationship he will do 'the right thing' and let her go. He will seem to do it quite easily, keeping his feelings under wraps. This is the man's way of coping with the situation – one that will be difficult for the mistress to handle as she will feel that he is not too bothered either way. This will hurt.

The lover may not be genuinely in love with the mistress, in which case he is just playing a game. 'Lots more where she came from' will be his reaction and he will therefore be quite dismissive of her sadness and seriousness of purpose. He will say things like, 'You were always free to go, whenever you wanted,' or 'I thought you liked our arrange-ment.' In a way this type of lover is more straightforward to deal with, as his behaviour will only strengthen the mistress's determination. It is harder, on the other hand, because she will have to face the fact that the love she imagined between them was a delusion. But at least she will be free.

When the leaving involves a conversation, the mistress should be very clear in advance whether they should drop all contact or whether they can call each other or even meet some time. There are no hard and fast rules here; either option can work successfully or fail dismally. It all depends on how the mistress comes to terms with the relation-ship, what happens in the heat of the break-up conversation, how strong she feels and whether his continuing presence will hinder or help her resolve to move on.

A letter, the last option, is open to interpretation and might not convey all that the mistress needs to say. As we mentioned earlier, it is also somewhat unsatisfactory as the mistress will not find out the lover's genuine feelings and witness his immediate reactions. She cannot be sure when or if he will receive it. The lack of a two-way conversation makes it easier for the mistress in the sense that she will not be put under emotional pressure, and once the letter is posted there is no turning back. If the mistress opts for this form of commu-nication, our advice is that the content of the letter should be precise. It should not leave any room for doubts (of the mistress's determina-tion) in the lover's mind. Moreover if she has chosen this method because she is afraid that meeting him or talking to him might shake her resolution, she should forbid any contact for a long time, six months at least.

Before she ends the relationship, it is worth questioning the lover as to what he thinks he would do, or how he would react, if she chose to leave. This can give the mistress some pointers for deciding how to leave, and when. The lover's comments are likely to be offhand as the situation is hypothetical, but they might help the mistress in deciding how to. He might not be truthful, sometimes for the best intentions, but if the mistress knows the lover well it might still help.

If after reading and considering all of the above the mistress still has doubts she should refer to Chapter 10 ('Staying in the Relationship'). If not, she should now be in a position of strength. She has accepted that the relationship is unlikely to progress in ways that will give her the life she wants. She understands that she will never come first in her current relationship, nor will she achieve any semblance of normality or security. She knows, however, that the longer she waits, the harder it will be to reach her life goals. She has, in short, determined to end the relationship and is convinced that her decision is right.

All that remains now is to do the deed and then weather the immediate aftermath.

The next day will be murder. She will be in a daze, unable to concentrate for more than short periods. Whereas the lover will probably keep busy and try not to think about what has happened, she will find this impossible. One of the mistresses we interviewed told us how she had to undergo two job interviews the next day and an important client visit the day after that. She did cope with these ordeals, with the help of short bursts of concentration, hiding uncontrollable tears at times (head down, pretending to read a report) and relying on her staff to carry her when she just lost track of a client conversation. She had to tell her staff what was happening and they came to rescue, understanding her situation. She was lucky.

The mistress will feel miserable, doubting her decision to have left him. She will never know whether he would have left his wife eventually if only she had stayed. She will never know if it would have been better for her to stay even if the relationship was not satisfactory and made her unhappy. She will feel her life is without purpose, and that she is just going through the motions every day. It will take time, sometimes a long time, before she can accept her new life without her lover and learn to enjoy the new freedom of her single status. Even when she does it may be a mixed pleasure.

The mistress who has gone through the process of ending the relationship has been strong and brave and has learnt a lot about herself, whether she succeeded or not. She will find that she is no longer drifting through life, but that she now knows what she wants. She will also have gained a new perspective on relationships, extramarital or otherwise. It is a sobering thought to realize how many people do not dare to do what is necessary in order to be happy, and stay in relationships that offer little apart from financial security and the approval of society. The mistress has not accepted the status quo, and has actively and courageously sought to change her situation, even it meant suffering a lot of pain. She is worth more than her lover, and she will be fine. Nature abhors a vacuum. Another love will come her way if and when the time is right.

12 Surviving Afterwards

He has finally gone. The centre of your life has disappeared, leaving a hole that you think only he can fill. If you made the break yourself, you feel that you have used up your last ounce of determination, courage and strength and have nothing left for yourself. If your lover walked out, you are bereft. Despite what you think or feel at this point, a successful future is attainable.

We are not going to trivialize your situation. We are not saying that the solution will be simple. This chapter will help you to explore and understand what you are going through and the way that you feel. It will look at the stages of grief that you must necessarily endure and the ways in which you can act to minimize their impact. It will offer short- and long-term advice and, we trust support a life that, now that you have been released from this unsatisfactory relationship, can only improve.

There is probably not an adult alive who has not had to cope with the end of a relationship or the death of a close relative or friend. The emotional phases that ensue are well documented and recognized, and no one will usually expect the injured party to be at their best afterwards. However, for the mistress, the situation is somewhat different and could be likened, in part, to the state of a battered wife when she finally manages to escape a relationship that has given her so much physical abuse. The mistress has been emotionally abused; the scars may not be visible, but he has damaged her just the same. The affair has caused her a great deal of pain. She has had to deal with most of this pain on her own and almost entirely without her lover's support. In order to heal, her unseen wounds will need time, and the support of people around her.

The most difficult situation for the mistress to manage is the one where she herself initiated the end of the affair. What makes this so tough is that in most cases she is still in love with the man she has left. Deliberately walking away from someone you love, or believe you love, is something that few people ever even have to consider. She walked away because she could see no other solution, because she had either run out of hope or just did not have the energy to continue. She did not, however, run out of love.

Most people will see the end of her relationship as something to celebrate rather than something to mourn and, instead of sympathy and support, she is more likely to encounter such statements as, 'You're better off without him.' Whether this is true or not is at first irrelevant. The mistress will not feel better off without him in the days, weeks and months immediately after the end of the affair.

Walking away is the easy part, just as giving up smoking for a day is easy. The hard part is working through her bereavement in the medium term. The stages she will go through, although not necessarily in this order, are disbelief, anger, grief, resolve and finally action.

At first grief will be intense and she must learn to handle it in whichever way is best for her. Some will postpone their pain by keeping frenetically busy, making sure they are not alone and planning new events and activities for their immediate futures. Others will draw the curtains and want to be alone. It is not for us to say which of these is best in the short term, but eventually each must express and deal with their misery and each must work towards the time when they can once again live a normal life.

Throughout the early days it is important that she tries to find the opportunity to talk with someone who understands or, at the very least, tries to understand. The ideal confidante would be someone who has endured the same situation, but the taboo nature of affairs means that other former mistresses may be hard to identify. Sometimes less personal contacts with organizations such as the Samaritans or Relate will provide a listener who may be able to offer a less judgmental perspective than close friends can.[1]

Initially she will miss him dreadfully, cry too much, sleep too little and continue to wonder whether she did the right thing by walking away. She will remember the quotation, 'He who does not love too much, does not love enough' and question the strength of her love. She will wonder if she is weak for not being able to endure the situation. She will question both her values and herself, and will keep revisiting the reasons why she felt she had to leave. She will dwell upon the last time she saw him, and while her head will concentrate on the bad times, her heart can only dwell upon the good.

She will feel a sense of shame, especially if she has seen clearly the foolishness of the relationship for the first time. She will wonder how she could have been so naive or so stupid to play second fiddle for so long, to ignore all the signs and to maintain her hope of a fairy-tale ending despite all the contrary evidence. She will remember all the friends who tried to warn her when she would not listen and see all the things they could see that she was blind to before.

She will wonder how he is coping without her and if he misses her at all. The cynic in us asks, 'Why wouldn't he?' He had a very good deal for a long time and now it is over. On the other hand, he may suddenly realize just how important she was to his life. This does not necessarily mean he will do anything about it. He knows what she wants – he always has – but he is unlikely to offer the incentives that would persuade her to go back to him.

Each time the telephone rings she will jump, simultaneously dreading and hoping for his voice on the other end of the line. She fears that she will never love this way again and then immediately fears the exact opposite. Her mind will be in turmoil as she fights to control her feelings; she strives to understand why, when she gave him her very best and accepted so little in return, he still did not want her. This last fact shows why, for most, the period directly after the break-up adversely affects her self-esteem so much. She was a bargain yet, even then, everything she was and did has been rejected.

It takes a while before the reality of her situation hits her. Given the sporadic nature of the relationship, she is used to enduring long periods without him. The longer the gaps have been in the past, the longer it takes before she truly realizes it is over. During this period most mistresses talk about a sense of unreality, difficulty in concentrating and lack of direction as they continue, often unawares, with the habit of waiting for him to call. And indeed he might call, although we have to say that this does not happen very often. But in case he does, she needs to think about her reaction. In the early days she is extremely vulnerable. There may be a time when it will be safe to talk to him again, but this is definitely not it. Each mistress harbours the dream that her lover might rush back into her life, declaring that he cannot live without her. This dream, along with all her other unfulfilled dreams, is simply another obstacle to be overcome. Hope is extremely persistent.

If the lover is going to make a play to win her back, he is most likely to do so shortly after the end of the relationship. It is almost as if he knows by instinct that this would be the best time – when she is at her weakest. He might plead, although this is rare. He might use the 'I'm sure we can work this out if we just talk about it' approach. He might make wild declarations of love and rash promises that he has no intention of keeping. Unless the mistress's decision is solid, any of these approaches might persuade her to change her mind. She wants to believe that he does care, and to learn this is often enough for her to reconsider her decision. However, the likelihood is that she will be going straight back into a relationship that, by her own admission, had become intolerable before and will soon become intolerable again.

She needs to remind herself why she left and, difficult though it may be, insist upon the changes that would make her return to him. It is better if she has thought this through before he calls. With her lover on the other end of the line, the mistress is rarely in the best frame of mind to make logical and rational decisions about her future. In the vast majority of cases, she wants him to leave his wife, and to go back to him for anything less than this decisive gesture would therefore be pointless and merely postponing the agony.

If he does not ring, then she might phone him, sometimes convincing herself that this is just going to be a one-off call, sometimes half hoping to renege on her resolve. It is quite possible that he will not want to resume the relationship. Many married men, even if they do value their mistresses and are hurt by the end of the affair, still have a sense of relief when it finally ends. This is especially true if they were not the ones who initiated the break. Their heads quickly gain control of the situation and the mistress will probably hear 'I guess it's all for the best' than 'Yes, please come back immediately.' In ending the affair, she has given him a breathing space to take stock and he is probably going to be sensible rather than reckless.

However, even if the relationship does resume, she will find that something fundamental has changed – at least for a while. Both will now realize that she is capable of walking away and she will have given her head a period of control over her emotions. She will have forced herself to look objectively at her situation and faced a number of painful home truths. This will make a difference to the way she behaves within the affair and she will find that she has a more balanced perspective on its management. In most cases, though, the break has begun. Unless something changes, she will leave again and, perhaps next time, leave for good.

If the relationship does not resume, most of her time will be spent in resistance during the first few weeks and months. She will resist her feelings, resist contacting him, resist the hope of a reunion and resist the urge to give up on everything. This is draining and makes planning and undertaking new ventures extremely difficult. If the affair was one of the many initiated in the workplace, she will have to handle the possibility of seeing him day after day. To an extent, the formality of the working environment will help her, but some mistresses have found these situations intolerable; some have even resigned. Although changing jobs should be considered only as a last resort, if it is not possible for her to move to a new department where all contact is minimized, she might find it both a relief and a therapeutic opportunity to seek new employment. This and any other changes she is able to make will help her to break the patterns that tie her to the habits of her past.

She can change her appearance – a new hairstyle or revamped wardrobe. She can switch round the furniture in her home or decorate her bedroom, removing as many reminders of him as possible. Often, most of the meetings occurred in her home, within her space. Everything she has can be associated with him. He has no such reminders: his house is free from her in a way that hers could never be free from him.

There will be time to reminisce, time to play the songs they shared and go to the places they used to visit. However, she will find it much easier to avoid anything that will remind her of the relationship while she is still in mourning. Some take the drastic measure of throwing all personal mementoes away; the more sentimental will find this untenable. So we at least recommend buying a large crate, packing everything away (including those letters!) and storing it in the attic. Later, when she is stronger, she can rediscover it and indulge her emotions to her heart's content.

Immediately after the break-up the mistress needs to force herself into action. Even getting out of bed can seem pointless. Some form of exercise is a must, as is socializing. If necessary, a visit to the doctor may be warranted to help her overcome her general sense of lethargy. There is nothing to be ashamed of in taking medical advice and remedies under such stressful circumstances. Above all, she needs to rest and find a way to relax.

The best thing she can do is look for diversions, something, anything to help take her mind away from the temptations she faces. Life for her is a bit like eating with no sense of taste. Therefore, new people and stimulating situations that lack the old associations should be fostered.

Support groups cater for a range of different addictions, but none exists to help mistresses and, in a sense their behaviour has addictive features. At the physical level, her body is habituated to the chemical changes wrought by the passion, as well as the fear and excitement of the affair. Furthermore, her major goal, of being with her lover permanently, has evaporated with nothing as yet to replace it. She has let go of the man but will find it much harder to let go of the dream.

Although most of the time avoiding her former lover will help, her emotional state will still make her want to stand up and say, 'Hi, my name is Judy and I'm in love with a married man' and receive the appropriate feedback of empathy and reasoned advice on how to kick the habit. It is important that if she wants to talk, reminisce or just cry, she can do so in a safe environment with a good and understanding listener. To try to suppress feelings totally is dangerous, for without an outlet they will build like a pressure cooker.

The grieving process lasts for as long as it lasts. For some, it might take only a few weeks, for others it might take years. We cannot stress enough the importance of forging a sense of self-belief during this time. The mistress has got to want to recover and has to believe that her life can flourish without her lover. This is not as simple as it sounds. Letting go is the hardest challenge she faces.

It helps if she gets angry, if she reminds herself of the bad times rather than dwelling on the good. This is not a state of mind to be preserved but to be used as a stepping-stone towards the restoration of her self-worth. Prolonged anger only leads to bitterness, which becomes corrosive over time; in the short term, however, better than she be angry with her lover for his behaviour than attack herself for her perceived failure.

She knows that her lover, even if he was one of the good ones, did not treat her very well. He accepted her love, knowing that he could offer little in return. He took little or no responsibility for her well-being. He constantly showed her, by word and deed, that she was not as important as his family, friends, job and society at large. In short, he treated her as a second-class citizen. She in her turn has to learn that she is worth more than that. She may have to admit that she was misguided, a fool even, but acknowledging such truths is a small price to pay for her freedom from an unequal and damaging partnership.

The initial signs of recovery are subtle. It begins on the first day the mistress does not think about him at all. On realizing this, she may be seized by a sense of alarm. Perversely, maintaining his importance allows her to hold on to the thought that he was actually worth all the heartache and that she was not wrong to love him. He has become valuable to her if for no other reason than that she has paid so dearly for him. As his impact on her life lessens, however, so does the importance of what he cost her. She has to face the fact that, in the end, she paid too much for too little. In short, she was cheated. Ultimately, all she needs to accept is simply that love makes fools of us all.

Building a positive future should be the former mistress's number one priority: new relationships for the single woman, a review of her marriage for the married one, visiting and socializing with new and old friends, initiating new activities and exploring new career horizons.

There are no hard and fast rules about new relationships. For some single mistresses, looking for a new partner as soon as possible proves to be most beneficial. Others prefer to wait. However, it is important for the former mistress to think about her attitude to new relationships as soon as she feels able. Some believe that they will never find anyone else. Some believe that they do not want anyone else. Some cannot wait to find a replacement. Some hope for a replacement – but not yet.

The women who does not believe she will ever find someone else is probably having grave doubts about her self-worth. It could be that she is older now and that most of her friends have already settled down and married. In fact, the older she is the harder it will be for her to recover. A younger woman is usually more robust and, being realistic, does have more options and more future in which to realize her dreams. A former mistress can easily convince herself that the only reason she managed to keep her lover was that she gave him every-thing for relatively little, thereby negating her positive qualities. This is understandable but misguided. Despite what she may think, the fact that her lover stayed with her for so long under such difficult circum-stances meant that he valued the relationship. Perhaps she was not aware of the price he paid, but it was there just the same. She lost him or left him because the odds were stacked overwhelmingly against her, not because she was worthless. Finding the self-confidence and self-belief she needs takes time, but the best way to achieve these ends is for her to spend time with other people, look for success elsewhere and not to shut herself away.

The woman who really believes that she does not want anyone else is usually still very much in love. Her defeatist attitude protects herself from further pain and affirms the depth of her feelings. When we love and love deeply, the feeling never truly disappears. All we can know is that, eventually, the pain of loss will fade if we allow it to, leaving in its wake a wonderful memory. There are grandmothers who will tell their grandchildren over a glass or three of sherry about that one great love that got away decades before. It is usually impossible to embark on a new relationship while still carrying the baggage of a previous one. It is unfair to both parties. Hackneyed though the saying is, time does heal all wounds, and often without warning and quite unexpect-edly, it becomes possible to love again – but first she must want to love again. Fear of failure and fear of pain will both inhibit her future. This happens to anyone who has been hurt, but eventually love demands that we find the courage to love again.

For those women who want to seek a new partner, numerous options can be explored no matter what their ages. Nothing is ever guaranteed, but marriage bureaux and newspaper advertisements, which no longer carry the stigma they used to, and new activities that increase the number of potential candidates, are all possibilities to investigate. True, the initial attempts may be half-hearted and the results sometimes discouraging, but it is still important to make the effort. We have heard many stories of women who have explored these avenues only to find their Mr Right living almost next door. Perhaps this works in a similar way to those apparently infertile couples who, having adopted a child, then manage to produce one of their own.

For the married ex-mistress, this is a time to examine her partnership with her husband. She should take a long hard look at her marriage and try to understand what her lover gave her that her husband did not. She needs to consider seriously what she believes is wrong and what, if anything, could be done to rectify the deficiencies she sees. She needs also to evaluate what is right about her marriage and in what respects her husband compares favourably with her former lover.

She needs to assess whether she still wants to maintain the marriage and, if so, the reasons why. These will help to give her the incentives she needs to effect the repairs and introduce new activities that might offer her the opportunity to help her find fulfilment. Above all, difficult though it may be, she needs to involve her husband in the changes. She does not have to confess the affair, but she does need to discuss their relationship and try to help him understand what she wants. As lack of closeness and communication are so often cited as major contributors to infidelity, now is a good time to start bridging the gaps that have opened up between them. Some married mistresses have argued that attempts to repair the damage would fall on deaf ears. But they will not know unless they try.

If her bridge-building efforts are rebuffed, she might need to ask herself whether the disadvantages of her marriage outweigh the advantages. If she does not believe she can make her marriage work as she would like, she could still consider leaving, even without her lover there to catch her. However, the vast majority of married ex-mistresses do stay with their husbands and manage to build acceptable, if not ideal, new lives with them. They usually find that this reality is often neither as rosy, nor as bad, as they thought it might be.

The former mistress has a problem that is not easily soluble. She can do many things to help speed her recovery and decrease her sense of helplessness, but essentially the solution will appear only after the appropriate amount of time has elapsed. Socializing and spending time with others is always beneficial, as is working to assist other people. Sometimes it is therapeutic to be able to deal with someone else's problems instead of her own, and numerous charitable and voluntary organizations would be only too pleased to receive the offer of her services. Provided her motivation comes from the desire to assist others, rather than solely to escape her own problems, she has much that would be of use. She had a lot of love and care to give and has learned much about relationships and the difficulties of recovering from emotional pain. She knows a good deal about what not to say, having been on the receiving end of much well-meant but unhelpful advice. She has learned a lot about herself. It is hardly surprising that many of the 'walking wounded' can be found in support organizations – people who have turned their negative experiences into positive expression and the opportunity to help others.

In addition, she should seek changes in her social life. This not only brings variety to her life but also helps her to destroy old patterns of behaviour. Opportunities abound. Evening classes, weekend residential courses and correspondence courses will combine acquiring new knowledge with the chance to meet fresh faces. The choice is enormous – from academic studies to aromatherapy and astrology, woodwork to creative writing, car maintenance to computer studies.

Sports, if she feels she has the energy, offer particularly good opportunities for meeting people and combine social life with exercise. Those who are unfit need not despair for such sports as shooting, archery, bridge and perhaps golf do not require any athleticism. The names of clubs can be found easily from the local library, council offices or telephone directories. It is often a good idea to enrol in a beginners' class as it is often easier to form an initial connection with people. Often the mistress is feeling under-confident and would find it difficult to walk into an already established group. If she can persuade a friend to accompany her, so much the better, but sometimes she needs the experience of exploring new avenues on her own.

The mistress may have neglected some of her existing friends during her particularly low times – or vice versa. Sometimes everyone (including her) gets fed up with listening to the same old problems, especially ones that have no obvious solution. However, she needs to signal her first signs of recovery as soon as possible, difficult though it may be for her to make the initial approaches. She often feels ashamed of the way she has behaved and fears that she appeared weak and pathetic in their eyes. Old friends often understand much more than we realize. They will help her, and probably much more readily, once they recognize her determination to restore herself to full fighting capacity. They will be relieved to see her looking and feeling better, which will also help them to address the sense of inadequacy they have been experiencing in not being able to make her feel better in the past. She will find it easier to listen to their concerns about her previous relationship than she did at the beginning and start to appreciate their negative views of her lover. The less emotionally involved she is, the more able she will be to agree with their assessment of her situation.

By adopting a completely unemotional view of what she has endured for the sake of her lover, she may be surprised that what seemed so tragic before now seems amusing. She will be able to recount with dry humour stories of how she sat by the telephone hour after hour – stories that at one time had all the hallmarks of a Greek tragedy. She will relate tales of her passivity with disbelief, suddenly realizing that her relationship only scratched the surface of who she was and what she was capable of being. Her incredulity and her ability to find humour in her past situation is all part of the healing process and helps others to relate to her more positively.

Spending time with others not only gives her something to focus upon other than her lover, it also gives her a reason for making an effort. A mistress we interviewed explained that, after the end of her affair, the only reason she got up in the morning was because she had to feed her cats, and at the beginning that was enough to ensure that she carried on with her life. It does not sound like much, but its importance to her recovery cannot be underestimated. While the mistress tries to put herself back into the centre of her life, it does not matter what her motivation is in the meantime.

If going to a club means that she will take care of her appearance; if owning cats means that she will get out of bed; these will be enough to sustain her during the difficult times. None should be too quick to judge the quality of these incentives. In time she will have other reasons; in time she will start to do things for herself, rather than for others.

The odds on recovery from a broken heart are excellent and stacked in the mistress's favour. She will know she is better from a number of key observations. She can think about him with smiles instead of tears. She can open the crate (or envelope, if he was less generous) in the attic and view the contents with curious nostalgia. She can visit the places they used to go without thinking about him at all. She could see him again without wanting him back – or could she? This is the last and most dangerous test.

Some mistresses never have to, and never want to, see their lovers again. They might have lost all feeling for them completely or ended up despising them. However, others wonder what it would be like if they met again and whether they could ever be friends. In most cases, developing a friendship after an affair is fraught with difficulty. It has taken the mistress much energy to exorcize the lover, and if she has done a good job, there will be little left for her to offer him. He, on the other hand, has almost invariably resumed his life with his wife. His former mistress can often present a dangerous reminder of his past infidelity and thus a threat to the regained equilibrium of his marriage. Any attempt to form a relationship again, no matter how casual, is often uncomfortable for both. Some lovers and mistresses do manage it, but it is fairly rare.

Moreover, any reunion has attendant dangers – much as 'just one cigarette' or 'just one small drink' can be dangerous for the former smoker or alcoholic. It is tempting for both to think that a meeting could be engineered without risk; but neither can be absolutely sure of the outcome. We know of a mistress who, after nearly ten years' separation from her lover, met him for a friendly drink and within four weeks had resumed her relationship with him – a relationship, we might add, that offered her no more than it did first time around. None was more surprised than she, who had thought herself immune. Each mistress must ask herself whether it is really worth the risk, no matter how small she perceives that risk to be.

However, for most, recovery is inevitable. The mistress has fought for her new life and has managed to extricate herself from a destructive relationship. She has overcome her sense of loss and recovered her self-worth. She has done something that few have done and is stronger for it. Whether or not she has a new relationship, she has learned much about love, what it is and what it is not, and can marvel at her capacity to feel for another human being while receiving so little in return. She has loved, she has lost and she has survived, like millions before her. She knows that emotional pain has no easy answers. If someone could invent a pill that we could take to make love go away, they would make a fortune. She knows that each must find their own way of approaching and dealing with their grief and that each must, and can, find their own way to build a new life.

13 Statistics

There are no statistics that tell us how many women are mistresses, their marital status, how long the relationships last or what the outcomes are. The majority of research available concentrates on adultery, usually defined as having sex with someone other than the spouse. No distinction is made between one-night stands and long-standing affairs. The questions asked in these surveys aim to define sexual attitudes and behaviour, how important fidelity is and how deadly the affair is for the married partners, not for the mistress.

The existing surveys vary greatly in terms of their statistical reliability, as most are not based on national probability samples and many interviewees are self-selecting. The data is sketchy mainly because both infidelity and adultery remain taboo subjects and do not attract the large-scale funding essential for taking representative surveys. It is not surprising that a self-selecting survey within a religious community and one printed in *Playboy* magazine would produce very different results. Most of these surveys have one thing in common: they ask no questions about the single mistress's circumstances or her views on the relationship.

This chapter endeavours nonetheless to make sense of the available statistics in the context of the mistress. We discuss several surveys, noting the sample and the type of questions asked and drawing probable conclusions. Official social-trends surveys and population statistics are then used to estimate the number of mistresses in the UK – an estimation made possible by accurate figures on how many women are single, divorced or married.

In the UK, the *Guardian* newspaper and ICM pollsters investigated fidelity, betrayal and affairs.[1] The survey found that people had different definitions of what constituted an affair. For some, a kiss and a cuddle, or even a close friendship, was enough to count. ICM therefore asked the respondents how many had ever had a 'close physical relationship' with someone else while they were married or living with someone. The answer was 27% of men and 15% of women, more than one in five on average. At the time when people started their first affair they had usually been married or living in a steady relationship for around seven years.

Not surprisingly, the survey found that the whole subject of infidelity is riddled with double standards, as only 5% thought it was acceptable to have a full sexual relationship with someone other than their spouse or steady partner against the average of 21% who had done so. Different wordings changed the results slightly: on average, 8% thought infidelity was acceptable, 19% said it was 'OK' to have affairs and 35% said they might have one if the opportunity arose.

There is a marked difference between the sexes. Of the 19% who found infidelity acceptable, 12% are men and 4% are women, and only 1% of women find infidelity acceptable. Men are also more likely to condone affairs and admit to them, and it would seem that there are a lot of men who have had a few affairs against a few women who have had a lot of affairs. According to men, their relationships last around a year, whereas women say theirs last twice as long. Other research has confirmed that men's views on what constitutes infidelity are different. They believe that a one-night stand or a visit to a prostitute does not amount to infidelity, while women feel it does.

According to the ICM study women are more emotionally involved in their affairs, a fact also confirmed by Annette Lawson's studies[2] into adultery in the 1980s. Both show that women have affairs because they feel compelled to do so by their emotions; secondly, because they felt they had grown apart from their spouses. They are also more likely to love their lovers. When asked how they felt about starting an affair, most men replied, 'With care, the affair would not harm my marriage'; in the second place, they were curious to know what sex would be like with someone else. Further, the ICM study found that only 38% of men professed any love for their lover, while 57% continued to love their wives or their partners. Only 22% of women are likely to feel the same way.

Men do not find out about 60% of their partners' affairs while women do not find out about 40%. Women enjoyed sex much more with their lovers than their partners, while this was less significant for men. Women also found that their sex lives with their partners got worse during the affair, while men actually found that theirs got better. Half the women claimed their lover used a condom at first to reduce the risk from AIDS against 33% of men, and women also claimed that their lovers used a condom for a longer period than men claimed to have used them. Despite the affair, 80% stayed with their respective partners. This is confirmed by other studies showing very similar figures.

The ICM/*Guardian* study interviewed a controlled sample of 596 adults aged between 22 and 55, either married, in a long-term relationship or recently separated. The results show significant and conflicting differences between the sexes in terms of length of the relationship, use of condoms and the like, and the conclusion drawn is that men are more boastful than women, who are more modest, even in an anonymous survey guaranteeing privacy. This may be so to an extent, but some conclusions are also drawn on the premise that the answers between the sexes in this population should match, which they don't. Fewer women claim to have had affairs, fewer in fact than is statistically possible. The likely reason for this is that single people[3] were not included in the sample unless they were recently separated. If 27% of men have affairs against 15% of women in this sample, that would indicate that 12% of men have a single woman as their mistress, unless of course few married women have affairs with hundreds of married men. Men also had a slightly higher number of affairs so this would tend to raise the figure. Some women may have their affairs with single men, which again will increase the number of single women as mistresses. We cannot of course exclude the possibility that members of both sexes are simply claiming to have had affairs even if they haven't, but it would seem irrational to do so in an anonymous survey.[4]

Annette Lawson's research on adultery in the UK in the 1980s was based on interviews with people who volunteered through articles in the *Sunday Times*, the *Guardian* and the *Sunday Mirror*. Her sample contained more married, separated and divorced people than single (never married) people in comparison to a national sample. The women in the sample were of a higher social class (mostly middle class) and had slightly fewer children than a national sample. Unfortunately for our purposes, her survey concentrated on adultery and the results fail to distinguish between a brief encounter and a long-term love affair. The questionnaire concentrates on people who are or have been married and asks no questions about the length of the affair, nor any details about the partner with whom the affair was conducted, that is, lover, mistress or party to a casual affair.

However, her findings include some interesting insights into how men and women feel about their extramarital relationships. Within the sample, she found that 66% of women and 68% of men in their first marriages had at least one adulterous liaison, and over half the men and 60% of the women had an affair by the time they were forty. The sexual needs of 44% of both men and women were said to be unmet in their marriages. Men, when questioned about the benefits of their extramarital relationship, placed 'sexual fulfilment' first and considerably higher than the next benefit, while women placed it equally with 'being loved' and 'friendship'. Sex stood out for men; only around half of men said that friendship and being loved mattered to them, whereas women are much less inclined to separate sex from emotion. Lawson also found, like many other studies, that women find multiple sexual partners more difficult to sustain than men do.

The reasons for engaging in extramarital affairs were often expressed by people in terms of feeling only half alive, half functioning, or practically dead within their marriages. Marriage was seen (by those who had been unfaithful) as bread and butter, shelter and commitment, children's lives and extended family, a practical investment of time, energy and money. One of her interviewees admitted that he might well have a death-wish, for his successful life – 'with a dependable and delightful if not very stimulating wife and two children whom I adore' – bored him and left him feeling already dead. Another said: 'Enough. It's my turn to fly.' Most people experienced both a lot of happiness and a lot of pain in their extramarital relationship, but the more affairs a person had the greater happiness they felt. 'Being alive' was the most important pleasure for two-thirds of women and half the men, while ending the relationship brought the greatest suffering to 40% of people.

According to several studies[5] a greater number of married men have affairs than do married women, and they also have more of them; some 40% of men have had at least four affairs, but only 25% of women have had as many. The difference in educational background between husband and wife and the changing role of women in society also appear to affect the trends. It is suggested that if the husband has a lower educational level than the wife, he will not occupy the traditionally 'superior' relationship to his wife and will have fewer extramarital relationships than is typical of other men; his wife will have more affairs than is usual. The key appears to be role reversal – the change of dominance from the male to the female.

Similarly, as women become more independent and more likely to be employed as managers, solicitors or doctors, the divorce rates are set to rise. Fewer women will be constrained by financial considerations and will be less likely to lack the self-confidence to leave an unsatisfactory marriage if they so wish.[6] Men might also find that a 'yes dear, no dear' housewife will become a thing of the past, as a third of women will go through university (by the year 2002) and many older women return to work and to adult education. This might also lead to more divorces and, potentially, to more mistresses, as the pool of eligible men diminishes because of their lower lifetime expectancy and a higher rate of remarriage amongst men.[7]

Furthermore, if current trends continue, there will be more women (there are already 1.2 million more women than men in Britain), who will be older, more independent, more likely to be living alone and more likely to be divorced (40% of marriages are predicted to end in divorce).[8] It would seem that we are following the demographic trends in the United States, where the number of unmarried men in their forties is half that of single women. When this is compounded with the traditional propensities for women to 'marry up' and for men to select younger women as partners, it is easy to see that more unmarried women might become mistresses. The number of eligible men in the right age group will be insufficient to meet the demand.

In a recent survey by a popular women's magazine, compiled in association with Relate, 66% of women admitted to having an affair, which tallies with Lawson's figures but far exceeds the 15% in the ICM study. The 66%, nearly seven out of every ten married women, is a very high percentage attributable to the self-selecting nature of the participants. Someone who has been or is involved in an affair is more likely to read an article about affairs and more motivated to answer a survey. Nevertheless, we gain some interesting insights into married mistresses.

An overwhelming majority of the women in this survey who had had affairs saw nothing wrong in their actions, whereas the opposite was true for those who were faithful themselves. Many women who had had affairs had surprised themselves by committing adultery; it was not something they set out to do. They also found they became less judgemental about extramarital affairs generally. Some 84% had no regrets about their infidelity, even though for one in ten it led to a breakdown of their marriages. Some felt that the affair boosted their self-confidence after years of mothering. Many experienced in their marriage a lack of love, affection and sometimes sex, which left them feeling alone and let down. Many felt guilty about having an affair, but few if any were seeking only sexual gratification. For these women the affair was often a lifeline out of an unsatisfactory marriage. Just one half had had one affair and only a quarter confessed to having had more than two. In order to agree with the ICM statistics on the average number of affairs, a quarter would have to have had five affairs on average.

Of those who had been unfaithful 70% said it was possible to love two men at the same time, while only 40% of those who had not had an affair agreed. A similar pattern was evident when respondents were asked whether marriage can survive an affair. Of those who had been unfaithful 60% thought it could, while only 33% of the opposite group agreed. Of the women who had never been unfaithful, 60% said their husbands had committed adultery, while 34% of the women who had had affairs said their husband had been unfaithful too. Of those 23% had done it for revenge, although lack of love and companionship were again quoted as reasons.

Other research that is based on self-selecting samples includes survey by such magazines as *Good Housekeeping, Cosmopolitan, Essence, Playboy, Christianity Today* and *Psychology Today*. Because the samples, questions asked and terminology vary widely, so do the results. Some factor in the number and duration of marriages, some don't, some even fail to check to which marriage the respondent is referring. The range of people admitting to having affairs in these surveys varies from 10 to 70%, and because of the often homogeneous samples, the results can be at different ends of the spectrum. The figures most quoted in the popular press and books on fidelity are taken from the mould-breaking Kinsey Institute research and Hite Report.[9] The former claims that half the men and a quarter of the women in his samples had committed adultery, and the latter claims 70% of both married men and women are adulterous after five years of marriage.

The biggest survey on British sexual behaviour, sponsored by the Wellcome Trust,[10] interviewed more than 20,000 people between 1990 and 1991, and found that 80% of Britons regard extramarital sex as wrong, which again is on line with the ICM study. Less than 5% of married men and less than 2% of women reported having had more than one sexual partner in the year before the interviews. This, of course, just tells us that married people are not having affairs continuously. In the United States the National Opinion Research Center (NORC) at the University of Chicago, has conducted sexual behaviour surveys based on national probability samples, but again these correspond to the ICM survey, in that they exclude single men and women. The infidelity rates from the NORC surveys are similar to those from the ICM study: around 20% for married men and 10% for married women.

One pattern remains constant no matter which survey one studies: around twice as many married men have affairs than married women. This pattern is clear from the early Kinsey studies of 1948 and 1953 through to those of Annette Lawson, ICM research and many others. We still cannot quantify the number of single men having affairs with married women, but we can assume that nearly half of married men's affairs are with single[11] women, who may have been married before. Other conclusions can be drawn. Love and affection are important for women in a different way than for men. Men are more able to remain detached from affairs, while women find it more difficult to sustain two partners, especially if those relationships are both sexual.

When interpreting any of the research done in the sphere of extramarital relationships. it is important to acknowledge that people's views are dependent on their circumstances, background and beliefs. According to the NORC study, people's views are dependent on whether they have had an affair themselves. In addition, people don't always act in line with the values that they hold, so drawing conclusions based on what people say might not give a true picture. Lastly, as the subject of extramarital relationships is both complex and affects many of our lives directly or indirectly, every article on infidelity and related research is inevitably coloured by the author's views.

Although there are no longitudinal studies (involving the same sample surveyed at regular intervals over a long period of time) about mistresses in particular, trends in sexual permissiveness have been researched since 1973 by social scientists in the United States. Marital status is one of the main circumstantial factors affecting a person's views. Those who are divorced or separated are more sexually permissive,[12] as are those who have never been married. In the first case, they may be disillusioned about marital fidelity as a result of their own experience and in the latter, they might have a self-interest in approving of extramarital relationships as they have less reason to be committed to marital fidelity. However, homosexuals are usually over-represented in the 'never married' category and this may affect the research results.

Predictably, those who are unhappy with life in general and their marriages in particular are more approving of extramarital relationships, as they probably feel that they have a right to seek some happiness somewhere. Men are more permissive and less unhappy with their marriages than women, who will initiate a separation from their partners more quickly than men with an equivalent degree of unhappiness, remain less faithful overall and have a first affair sooner than similar men. Whereas many men – even if they take a mistress – will remain with the family unit for the sake of responsibility and social status, whether bored or otherwise unfulfilled, many women need emotional balance and will seek happiness elsewhere.

Other groups who are more permissive include those who are better educated, earn a high income, have a less religious upbringing, belong to middle and upper classes or are city dwellers. Education seems to promote liberality and more progressive thinking. Higher classes tend to be more modern and cosmopolitan in their outlook, and city dwellers have a less traditional outlook in general.

All these factors are well supported by several studies conducted between 1973 and 1989. Most are independent predictors of sexual permissiveness, but some are stronger than others. Education seems to play a stronger role than income, so material conditions are not necessarily important. Unhappy marriages have a significant correlation with extramarital relationships. Widows are less permissive than those who are divorced or separated. Whether having a sexual partner increases happiness or not is difficult to judge. Those reporting a sex partner besides their spouse are less happy than married persons with no other partners, but it may be that the conflict of living two lives creates more unhappiness in itself. However, none of the surveys makes this correlation. Sexual permissiveness in general has increased while people are not particularly happy with the change.

Predictably, a great majority of those who are unfaithful report that extramarital relationships are not wrong at all, and only around 10% of those who regard infidelity as always wrong have been unfaithful themselves. This general consistency between sexual behaviours and attitudes needs to be tempered by the appreciable number of people who report sexual behaviour at odds with their expressed values. This means that unless these two factors are correlated in a study we may draw the wrong conclusions.

Population statistics provide an important backdrop to all these figures. The population of the UK is 58.4 million. Of these 29.8 million (or 51%) are females and 28.6 million are males, so the sexes are fairly equal in number. There are 35.6 million aged between sixteen and retirement age, and around 21 million married. Some 14.6 million are not married, and of those 2.56 million cohabit, 5.5 million live alone, some 1 million are lone parents and more than 6 million share a house. This means there are 10.5 million married men and women and 7.6 million unmarried women, of whom 1.28 million cohabit.[13]

According to the Office of National Statistics (ONS) projections, by the year 2016 the number of marriages will have declined by one million and the proportion of all the other groups will have increased. The number of those who cohabit is estimated to increase by a million, lone parents will reach 1.2 million and the number of people living on their own will be 8.5 million. Factors causing the high increase in the number of single people are greater numbers of elderly, more independence among the young, people staying single for longer and rising divorce rates.

The trends are clear. Further study of these statistics shows that not only are divorce rates on the increase but the number of marriages is on the decline. People who divorce stay married on average for around ten years and divorce around the age of thirty-five. The number of divorces represents 1.39% of the married population, around 150,000 couples every year. Half the women who divorce find their standard of living has fallen and only 30% receive maintenance from a former husband, although two-thirds have dependent children. Only 6% remarry within a year, although 15% start living with a new partner during that time.

We have no statistics on the class, age or income structure of mistresses, nor do we know how many are divorced or have children. However, we can analyse the infidelity figures to help us approximate the number of mistresses. If we take the ICM results: out of the 11.78 million men and women who are either married or cohabit, 3.15 million and 1.75 million respectively, have affairs. This means that 1.4m single women, making up the shortfall, are mistresses. We are not taking into account the fact that some married women will have affairs with single men. It is also possible that a few married women have a lot of affairs, but this is not borne out by the studies. If we assume that approximately a quarter of married women have affairs with unmarried males, the number of unmarried mistresses could be conservatively estimated as 1.85 million. This represents 29% of not married women, nearly one out of every three, and a total of 3.62 million mistresses altogether, or 20% of all women between sixteen and retirement age.

We could look at this differently. Men who have affairs have 2.39 on average, whereas similar women have 2.17. Again, we do not know whether a married man would generally have affairs with married women or single women only, or in what proportion, if both. Multiplying 3.18 million affairs by 2.39 equals 7.6 million affairs altogether; for married women, the equivalent total is 3.8 million. It follows that even if all married women's affairs were with married men that still leaves 3.8 million affairs with no married woman counterpart, unless of course people have repeat affairs with the same person. We cannot, however, take the figure of 3.8 million for granted, since we do not know how many affairs single women have. Another probable inaccuracy is borne out of the fact that divorced people are usually not part of representative samples. It could be argued that they may have had more affairs on average than the married group – a possibility could again be distorting the figures.

Using the same logic, we could choose to believe some of the higher figures and take a median of several surveys, roughly equating to 50% and 25% infidelity rates for married men and women respectively. The results for this exercise are mind-boggling as this would mean that potentially 7.9 million affairs involve unmarried or uncohabiting women, a statistic immediately falsified by the fact that there are only 6.39 million altogether. The figures could only be true if the number of affairs by some single people were extremely high or if people count recurrent affairs with the same person as separate affairs. We just don't know, but on balance it seems likely that the ICM figures are more accurate.

All in all, drawing conclusions from these statistics is a perilous business, a broad estimate at best. What they do tell us for sure, however, is that the differences between the sexes are as pronounced in this area as in many others – that married men are much more prone to having affairs than married women, and that significant numbers of single or divorced women have affairs. But until social scientists conduct representative surveys on the subject of infidelity many unanswered questions will remain.

14 Personal Case Histories

We interviewed a large number of people in depth during our research for this book. Some of the stories we heard moved us, others surprised us, but they all made us think. It appears that very few mistresses escape unscathed from their affairs. However, the ways in which they view their experiences vary considerably.

We asked a representative sample to tell their stories, in their own words, and are extremely grateful for their kind permission to reprint them. We have changed names and some personal details to protect those involved, but nothing else. They make interesting, and sobering, reading.

Janet: personal assistant (married, no children)
I think Peter just swept me off my feet. I met him when I was only twenty-five – I was single then and he was some ten years my senior, so charming and considerate. We had so much fun. He would take me out to lovely restaurants, send me flowers, presents. We would go sailing or just walk in a park, it didn't matter – I felt I was really looked after and I felt safe. But it wasn't that simple.

It is difficult to explain. I am not sure that I loved him – at least, when he offered to buy me a flat and set me up as his mistress I somehow felt that this was not for me. I felt degraded. It was a hard blow in a sense, because I had thought he really cared for me and I could not understand why he didn't leave his wife and be with me. He just said he wouldn't. Another problem was that I had a boyfriend, too, with whom I had been living for the past seven years. This relationship was fine, but I didn't really love him and avoided the times when he wanted to speak about marriage and children. I didn't leave him because I couldn't afford it and I didn't want to be alone.

I suppose I learnt a lot from Peter, and I owe him for making me realize what I wanted out of life. He also supported me financially if I was a bit short, bought me dresses and jewellery, but I found that this wasn't enough: what I really wanted was to be married to someone I loved. Peter said he loved me but would never leave his family. Luckily, I then met James, whom I married, and we are very happy together.

I still think about Peter – he was so different and I think we had something special. It was difficult to leave him, especially as he was quite blasé about it. My love for James is real, but if I had a choice it would be Peter every time. This sounds dreadful, but James is so dependable, so unadventurous and yet adoring, that sometimes it makes me want to scream. Peter gave me a challenge, always surprised me and we made such a couple. I miss him. But I know James will make a good husband and I have made the right choice. I hope.

Ruth: accounts manager (married, no children)
I was single when I met Paul and, no, he's not my current husband. We met at work. The men outnumbered the women by about ten to one and there was always a lot of flirting, but nothing serious. I'd always told myself that I'd never go out with a married man and that women who did so were stupid and asking for trouble. It appears I was wrong on the first count but right on the second.

Paul was a charmer. He had a bit of a reputation at the office but he was always kind and considerate with me. In fact, he never flirted with me at all – which surprised me. I don't know when I first realized that I was attracted to him, but I do remember missing him one summer when he'd gone away on holiday. One day he asked me out for a drink and I went. The rest followed on so naturally that not once did I ever consider I was doing anything wrong. All my high ideals about staying away from married men just went out the window. I'm more realistic these days. I now believe this could happen to anyone, no matter what they say to the contrary.

The affair became extremely serious for both of us, and after about six months Paul talked of leaving his wife. He said he could not bear to be away from me and that the double-life was driving him crazy. I'd be lying if I said I tried to persuade him to stay with his wife. I was totally in love with him and blind to the consequences to all of us, particularly to the effect that this would have on his wife. Love seemed like an excuse to do the inexcusable.

He did leave. One Saturday morning there he was on my doorstep looking tired and miserable. There had been an awful scene at home and his wife had been distraught. Then followed the most painful week of my life. His parents came around and tried to persuade him to go home. They visited his wife and acted as go-betweens. He felt so guilty and we were both so unhappy. Then, only seven days after he had arrived, he went back to his wife. He said that he didn't love her but that he could not live with the guilt.

I'd really thought I had found the love of my life and, more importantly, that I was lucky enough that he loved me in return. Then I lost it all – but we came so close.

I moved jobs shortly afterwards and Paul still tried to contact me, but I couldn't talk to him or see him – it was all too painful. Most people would say he did the right thing. Perhaps he did, I really don't know any more. What's right? To follow your heart or your head? Seems to me that people get hurt whichever path they take.

I'm married now to a wonderful, kind man and I love him very much, but not with the passion I had for Paul.

Anna: housewife (married, two children)

I had been married for ten years when I had my first affair. My husband was the only man I'd ever slept with and then I met Jacob. The relationship with him grew slowly at first, but after a few months it was obvious we were heading towards an affair. This really bothered me, so, although it sounds naive, I went home and told my husband. He surprised me – he said that I should get it out of my system and that he was glad I'd told him. So I went ahead.

At first it was amazing, great sex and excitement, and I can't remember exactly when I knew that my feelings were changing, but eventually I knew that I wanted to be with Jacob permanently. Jacob was married too – he'd said he would never leave his wife, but I didn't believe him. I suppose it was all a mess. I would have left my husband but there seemed no point if Jacob stayed with his wife. I kept resolving to end the affair but could never find the strength.

Meanwhile, my husband admitted that he had started an affair with a woman at work. I often wonder whether he'd had affairs before and just never told me, and that was the reason he was so ready to let me be unfaithful. He says not, but I'm still not really sure. I could go into all the details of the pleasure and the pain of my relationship with Jacob, but there seems no point. Eventually he wanted out and the affair ended – I'd got too close and had stopped being fun. He was so callous and cold, it was such a shock. Unfortunately, my husband's affair seemed to be going from strength to strength and I was scared that I'd lose him too.

It sounds horrible now that I'm writing it down, but even though I didn't really love my husband in the same way any more, I couldn't face the prospect of being on my own. I didn't feel able to ask him outright to end his affair, he'd never asked me to end mine. So in the end, I got him back by getting him to feel sorry for me. It was easy. I was still pining for my lover so at least the misery was genuine. I told my husband that I'd ended my affair because I'd realized how important my marriage was to me. My husband knew I was depressed, but he presumed it was because I was upset by his affair. I think this flattered his ego. I wonder what he would have done had he realized the truth. But it worked and he left his mistress.

We tried to make a go of our marriage and I suppose you could say we succeeded, but it never was the same. We've been married twenty years now and have two children – they keep me sane. I've had several lovers and so has my husband. We're still together, but sometimes I still cry myself to sleep when I remember Jacob.

Jane: management consultant (single, no children)
I have known Ray for eighteen years and have loved him for seventeen of those. He was married when we met and he is still married now. I was single when we met and I am still single now. What amazes me so much is that I can honestly say that I'm truly glad I met him.

Our relationship has developed and changed considerably over the years, but he still fulfils me physically, emotionally and mentally. We have parted, sometimes at his instigation, sometimes at mine, but something always manages to bring us back together again. It's still painful at times, but it's easier for me now. Perhaps you just get used to the pain. We've become good friends, admire and respect each other and we've learned so much about ourselves during this relationship.

I know he loves me, but I also know he loves his wife and family, especially his children. In the early days, I desperately wanted him to leave his wife and be with me – but this no longer seems so important. I'm more secure now and I don't need him to prove his love in this way – besides, I couldn't live with the pain it would cause. I still harbour some pretty impressive dreams, but our relationship is different to a marriage and offers a special kind of personal freedom for both of us. I do understand his situation, probably better than he thinks I do, and I know how difficult it must be for him sometimes.

People are always asking me why I don't leave him. It's as if they expect love to be some kind of business deal and they think I'm not getting good value for money. Love's not like that. He's a special and passionate man, funny, intelligent and a remarkable mixture of strength and weakness. He's never tried to change me (and I'm not the easiest person in the world to get along with) and far more tolerant generally than I'll ever be. He loves me for myself and no one has ever done that before.

Regrets? I have a couple worth mentioning. I wish I'd met him five years earlier, before he got married, and I wish I could have had his child. I would have been a good mum. But, all in all, I would not have missed knowing this man for the whole world – he's been worth it all.

Jean: artist (single, no children)

I met Alex at work fifteen years ago. I was on the rebound from a long-term relationship and had decided to pull my socks up, stop moping about and at least pretend that I didn't have a care in the world. It was when I was in this highly ebullient and artificial mood that I first met Alex. The sexual chemistry was instantaneous. I knew he was married, but I thought, What the hell, I need cheering up, so why not? That was possibly the single most stupid and naive decision of my life and I often castigate myself, since in that moment I probably ruined my future in all sorts of ways I couldn't even contemplate at the time. Many would say I deserved all I got – perhaps they're right.

How can I summarize the seven years we spent together in a few sentences? It all went wrong is a good way to begin. We fell in love with each other, or rather he said he loved me. He wouldn't leave his wife, despite the fact that she was also having an affair. He left me and then came back again. I left him and then I went back again. Two people who appeared to love each other, who could not be together – it seemed such a waste. Looking back now, I know he hurt me a lot and I just stood there and took it. I just kept making allowances for the fact that he was married, but he made no allowances for the fact that I was on my own. It was a cruel and unequal partnership and eventually I knew I had to leave him for good. That was hard.

It was triggered by an event in my life that caused me to need his support. Up until then, I'd maintained my independence, trying not to ask for too much, but the first time I truly needed him he let me down. I was forced to see that, despite what he said, he didn't love me because he didn't take care of me. I realized that he'd never be there when I needed him. I knew that if I continued to let him take so much from me without giving very much in return, the relationship would ultimately destroy me. I ended the affair by letter – I could never have done it face to face. It was the single most difficult thing I had ever done in my life, because, despite everything, I never stopped loving him.

Afterwards was terrible. It took me about three years to recover properly. My friends were terrific; I don't think I could have managed without them. It was a long time before I wanted another relationship, but eventually I met someone else who restored my faith in men and in myself.

I don't believe I will ever love anyone else the way I loved Alex, but perhaps that's no bad thing. It was not a very healthy kind of love.

Louise: business consultant (divorced, one child)

I met Richard over twenty years ago. I was a divorced, single mother with a young son. He was eight years younger than me, married with no children. There was a very warm attraction from the beginning; we were friends at first and then, during the first year, a physical attraction developed and we became lovers. The years we spent together were some of the happiest I have ever experienced, but also some of the most hurtful I have ever endured. Even now I know some of the scars are still there, but the knowledge that I was once loved the way I was is also still there. All the happenings, both fantastic and traumatic, have shaped my life. As I write this, both the nadir and zenith of my emotions are still extremely vivid.

During the first year of our relationship, Richard battled deeply with wanting to live with me but knowing he should stay with his wife. I told him that maybe he should live on his own for a while, not see either of us, try to sort his feelings out and then make a decision. He did leave his wife and lived alone for a while, but came to see me practically every day. After a few weeks he came to me and said he had made a decision, to go back to his wife. He said he loved me even more but felt that his wife was not able to live alone, whereas he believed I was capable of handling life on my own. He went back to his wife and we did not see each other for about six weeks, apart from, most unfortunately, having to meet on a business basis. We both worked for the same company. Then, one Sunday, he rang and asked me to meet him in an hour. I met him and he opened the car door to show me all his personal possessions packed inside. I took him back.

A week after he moved in he was very depressed and said he felt he should go back to his wife again. We talked into the night; I told him he had to make a decision and commit to it because he wasn't being fair, or even honest, with anyone. After much turmoil, he decided to stay. His wife initially was very upset; however, during our first year together, she divorced him and remarried.

I knew it was not going to be easy and I felt partly responsible for allowing the affair to develop. But I felt sure we could be happy because one element was in no doubt – we both loved each other.

The years we were together were very exciting but also very turbulent, and I came to understand that he had never truly committed himself to me. My trust and belief in him started to diminish as it emerged that he was lying, gambling, drinking heavily and was also unfaithful to me with one of my friends. I supported him through all this and tried desperately to help him. He never really settled and sadly we are no longer together.

For a year after we broke up, I thought I was handling everything fairly well, but then I fell apart and hit rock bottom and felt a great sense of loss of 'what could have been'.

I am now in my late fifties and have been married, divorced and had relationships of different intensities, but I know Richard has been the only man in my life who truly loved me in a way no other man has ever done.

Virginia: management consultant (divorced, no children)
I met David in a party at a very difficult time when I was both divorcing and unemployed. I wasn't really looking for anybody and hardly noticed him at all, although I probably said hello, how are you and nice to meet you. He called me the next week and asked me out for a drink. I couldn't remember who he was, but he sounded nice and I thought I could do with some diversion.

We went out for dinner and nothing much happened. He was charming and made me feel at ease; I enjoyed the evening, but I didn't think it would lead to anything. We agreed that he would come for dinner the following week, and then it happened. After the meal (I made no special effort), as I was clearing the table, he asked me to kiss him, saying he had been thinking about it all evening. There was suddenly this electricity between us. As I returned to the kitchen, he coolly said that he was married and would never leave his wife. I did not know. I hadn't thought to ask. He didn't wear a ring. I did not know what to think.

At our next meeting he carried me to the bedroom and took his clothes off in front of me before I could even react. I can still visualize this and remember how it excited me. We made love, which was tremendous, and I was hooked. I fell in love.

We have continued our relationship ever since, through good times and bad, going on five years now, and have both slowly understood and accepted that we truly love each other. We talk with each other nearly every day, he stays with me once a week or so and we have had some brief holidays together.

Maybe he is the only man for me; I don't know. What I do know is that I love him like I have never loved anybody else. Even if we are very close and talk about everything, I still don't understand or accept how he can love me and stay with his family. I know he is bored with his life, that he would rather be with me, but I also know that he feels he has made a commitment to his wife and children he cannot break. Maybe he is a hypocrite, maybe he is selfish and maybe he does not want to see the facts, but we are so happy and comfortable when we are together. Too happy. My fear is that I am slowly destroying myself for this love, as I cannot continue much longer. Every time he leaves a part of me dies. I didn't want to leave him, but I knew I must.

It's all in the past now. We had dinner in my garden one warm evening in August. I had prepared a barbecue, set the table with flowers and candles and opened a bottle of wine. He knew that I was leaving him before I said anything, just by the way I looked and behaved. In the morning he was silently holding my hand and nearly in tears. I asked him to promise me three things: that he would sort out what he wanted out of life and learn to enjoy what he has, that he would give me first refusal if he was ever free and that he would call me if he was planning to 'appear on my doorstep'.

We have seen each other a few times since, and talk to each other now and again. I haven't really given up on him yet and I miss him terribly. I go through the motions every day, and hope that he will be on the doorstep or that I have fallen out of love. Neither has happened yet.

Pamela: retired (divorced, three children)
I should never have married. There's something about my character that automatically rebels against convention – even now when my hair is grey and I should know better. I have three great children so I'm glad about that, but generally speaking I should have stayed single. But that was difficult to do when I was younger, and I didn't have enough self-confidence at that time to buck convention.

My affair started following my divorce; I'd been married for eighteen years. I was demob-happy and the last thing I wanted was another restrictive relationship. I wasn't particularly looking for a married man; in fact I would have preferred a single one; but when you're over forty the choice is extremely limited – there are not a lot of eligible bachelors around and I didn't think I could face mothering a younger lover. It's strange how many wonderful women I know who live on their own – but no men. I believe that women are so much better at coping on their own than men (and therefore a lot less likely to compromise just to find a partner).

I met Jack at a party. He was charming, a good conversationalist and he made me laugh. He had been married for twenty odd years and had never been unfaithful before – well, that's what he told me.

I enjoyed every minute of our time together. It was like a dream come true. He didn't want to leave his wife and I didn't want him to either. He wasn't possessive and nor was I. He never questioned what I did when he didn't see me and, in short, he was completely different to my ex-husband. I loved the freedom, the excitement and the honesty, but we never actually fell in love with each other. It was more like having a best friend with the occasional bedroom scene for added interest.

The affair ended at my instigation, although Jack and I are still incredibly good friends. It seems that I do want more depth than the affair offered, but it was a great way of restoring my self-esteem and removing the cobwebs of my marriage.

I'm now with a wonderful man – he's divorced too and we're both determined to make this work. Friends of mine who've had affairs seem to have been extremely badly hurt, but then they didn't really want an affair – they wanted a marriage. I suppose I've been extremely lucky.

Trudi: teacher (married, two children)
Karl and I met at evening classes and became good friends over a period of about six months. He'd been married for five years and often talked about his wife; he seemed to be very happy at home. I'd been on my own for about eighteen months following the end of a long relationship. During that time I'd learned how to cope and was enjoying being single again. Initially Karl was just another friend and then something changed or rather I sensed that something had changed. It wasn't so much what he said but subtle things – looks, touches and those strange silences – that made me suspect that he wanted more than just friendship. I mentioned it to a close friend and we agreed that the last thing I needed was an affair with a married man. So I decided to ignore the signals and behaved as usual.

I remember the evening it all began so clearly. Karl and I were sitting in the cafeteria at the college when he leaned across the table, took both my hands in his and said, 'Trudi, I want to sleep with you.' It wasn't a surprise, but I went through all the usual protests despite the fact that, although I didn't say so at the time, I knew I wanted him too. I turned him down because that's what I was supposed to do; it was an automatic response. I knew, however, that if we continued to meet it would only be a matter of time before I changed my mind. I couldn't handle the situation at all so I stopped going to the classes and even changed my telephone number.

Two weeks later, on a Thursday evening, I answered my front door to find him standing there. I'd been so miserable without him. We talked for ages and that night, for the first time, we made love – and the affair began. I don't think either of us were prepared for the intensity of our feelings. It was difficult, but neither of us could bear the thought of ending it.

His wife found out eventually. Someone told her and to this day I don't know who. She gave him an ultimatum: 'Her or me'; he chose his wife. My world fell apart. I'd lost my best friend and the man I'd grown to love so much. I was angry with myself for getting into the situation and incredibly upset but I didn't do anything to try to persuade him to stay. Afterwards friends tried to help but nothing could fill the emptiness.

Then a miracle happened. Three months later, he called me at work and asked if I'd meet him for lunch. I did and the rest is history. He said he couldn't go on with his marriage, he was sorry he'd hurt me and he wanted me back.

We've been married for twenty years now and have two children. We found it really difficult to live with the guilt that continued long after his wife remarried but, despite this, we've never stopped loving each other. My head still tells me at times that what we did was wrong – but my heart still refuses to believe it.

References

1 The Mistress – Definition and History

1. Survey by *The Times*, 1990–91
2. 35 for women, 38 for men. *Financial Times*, 21 Aug 1995, p.5.
3. 'Divorcees who live in dread of getting old' by Sonia Purnell, *Independent*, 1995.
4. UK Marriage and Divorce Statistics 1993.
5. Laurel Richardson, *The New Other Woman: Contemporary Single Women in Affairs with Married Men* (Free Press, New York: 1995).
6. *Adult Data* (Department of Trade and Industry: July 1998).
7. The Executive Club of St James, 'Your Questions Answered' (material sent to prospective members).
8. Executive Introductions.
9. General Household Survey (ONS: 1996). Sample: 5067 women aged 16–19.
10. *Daily Express*, 8 February 1996, 'This cheating art' (review of Dr Robin Baker's *Sperm Wars*) & Annette Lawson, *Adultery*, pp.35–6.
11. *Cosmopolitan* survey (1982).
12. Stephen Brook, *The Penguin Book of Infidelities* (Penguin: 1994).
13. Helen Fisher, *Anatomy of Love*, p.321 (Touchstone Books: 1993).
14. Suzanne Frayser (1985).

4 The 'Wanton Mistress'

1. Zick Rubin, 'Measurement of Romantic Love' (*Journal of Personality & Social Psychology:* 1970), 16(2), 265–73.
2. V. Adams, 'Getting at the heart of jealous love', (*Psychology Today:* May 1980).
3. J. Bowlby, *Attachment and Loss* (Penguin: 1971).
4. General Household Survey (ONS: 1997).
5. Dr J. Johnson & Dr C. Ratey, *Shadow Syndromes* (1996).

5 The Lover

1. Annette Lawson, *Adultery: An Analysis of Love and Betrayal* (OUP: 1988).

6 The Married Mistress

1. *A Guide for the Married Man* (1967).

8 Legal and Financial Considerations

1. Burns v. Burns [1984] 1 CH 317 CA.
2. Hammond v. Mitchell [1992] 2 A11 ER 109.
3. Coombes v. Smith [1987] 1 FLR 352.
4. Thomas v. Fuller-Brown [1988] 1 FLR 237 CA.
5. Lloyds Bank plc v. Rosset [1991] AC 107.
6. Wayling v. Jones [1995] 2 FLR 1029.
7. Midland Bank plc v. Cooke and Another [1995] 2 FLR 915.
8. Inheritance (Provision for Family and Dependants) Act 1975 (I(PFD)A).
9. Currently £75,000 if there are children, £125,000 where there are close relatives but no children.
10. AEA 1925, s46(I).
11. I(PFD)A 1975, The Administration of Estates Act (AEA) 1925, s46(I).
12. I(PFD)A 1975.
13. The Family Reform Act (FLRA) 1969.
14. FLRA 1987, s19.
15. FLRA 1969.
16. FLRA 1987, removal of s20.
17. Under Schedule 1 to the Children Act 1989.
18. A v. A (a minor: Financial Provision) [1994] 1 FLR.
19. Phillips v. Peace [1996] 2 FLR.
20. 1996, part IV.
21. Housing Act 1988, Housing Act 1985, Rent Act 1977, Children Act 1989.
22. Grant v. Edwards [1987] 1 FLR 87.
23. Australian Capital Territory Domestic Relationships Act 1994.
24. i.e. income that is earned, not income from investments etc.
25. Also dependent on other parameters like her age, current rates, and whether she smokes.
26. Decreasing term insurance will pay out the remainder owed in case of death, whilst the level term insurance will pay out the total amount borrowed, i.e. there may be a surplus.
27. This will be changed from year 2000, but will not be retrospective.
28. The growth assumption made by the Government Actuary in calculating the possible pay-out.
29. These figures are for guidance only.

9 The Options

1. *Cosmopolitan* survey 1982.
2. Affairs happen in 50% of marriages, 40% of these end in divorce but only 10% marry their mistress/lover.

11 Ending the Relationship

1. *The Sunday Times,* 31 August 1997, 'Flying into trouble'.

12 Surviving Afterwards

1. Any mistress reading this book who feels she has no one to talk to, can write to us, care of our publishers and we will do our level best to help in whatever way we can.

13 Statistics

1. *Guardian,* 1995.
2. Annette Lawson, *Adultery* (Oxford University Press: 1988).
3. Never married, divorced or widowed.
4. For further analysis on the unreliability of available surveys see Annette Lawson, *Adultery*, pp.75–7.
5. A. Lawson, Gebhard, Blumstein & Schwartz, ICM.
6. Helen Wilkinson and Melanie Howard, *Tomorrow's Women* (Demos: 1997).
7. Laurel Richardson, *The New Other Woman: Contemporary Single Women in Affairs with Married Men* (Free Press: 1985).
8. Helen Wilkinson and Melanie Howard, *Tomorrow's Women* (Demos: 1997).
9. Shere Hite, *The Hite Report* (Macmillan: 1978).
10. Intended to help doctors to stop the spread of Aids.
11. Never married, divorced or widowed.
12. Confirmed by A. Lawson.
13. General Household Survey, Dept of Environment, Government Actuary's Dept, General Register Office (NI and Scotland) (ONS: 1997).

Bibliography

Adonis, Andrew, 'Fewer couples marry but record numbers divorce', *Financial Times*, 23 August 1995

'Adultery: What you told us', Relate, 1995

'An affair to remember', *Essence*, July 1990

'Another world: More and more single women are opting for affairs with married men . . .', *Psychology Today*, 1986

Blumstein, Philip and Schwartz, Pepper, *American Couples* (William Morrow, New York, 1983)

Botwin, Carol, '16 ways to predict it you'll have an affair', *Redbook*, February 1994

Botwin, Carol, *Tempted Women* (Vermillion 1994)

Bowlby, J., *Attachment and Loss, Volume 1: Attachment* (Penguin, 1971)

Brook, Stephen, *The Penguin Book of Infidelities* (Penguin, 1994)

Caine, Naomi and Davidson, Helen, 'Men still behave badly over women's salaries', *The Sunday Times*, 26 January 1997

Colgrove, Melba, *How to Survive the Loss of a Love* (Leo Press, 1976)

Connor, Steve, 'Love is . . . three electrical circuits . . . er, that's it', *The Sunday Times*, 16 February 1997

Curphey, Marianne, 'Loving Britons favour fidelity', *The Times*, 1995

D'argy Smith, Marcelle, 'This cheating art', *Daily Express*, 8 February 1996

Darling, Lynn, 'A rake's progress', *Esquire*, June 1994

Driscoll, Margarette, 'Are children worth the candle?', *The Sunday Times*, 16 March 1997

'Faithful attraction', *Good Housekeeping*, June 1990

Fallis, Greg, 'Is your man cheating? How to be your own detective', *Cosmopolitan*, March 1983

Family Policy Studies Centre Bulletin, The, Family Policies Centre, 1995

Fisher, Helen, *Anatomy of Love: Natural History of Monogamy, Adultery and Divorce* (Touchstone Books, 1993)

French, Marilyn, *The Women's Room* (Summit Books, 1977)

Gascoine, Jill, *Addicted* (Corgi, 1994)

Gebhard, Paul, 'Sexuality in Post-Kinsey Era' (Galton Lecture, 1978) in W. Armytage, R. Chester and J. Peel (eds), *Changing Patterns in Sexual Relations* (Academic Press, New York, 1980)

General Household Survey, Office of National Statistics, 1996 & 1997

189

Greeley, Andrew, 'Marital infidelity', *Society*, May–June, 1994

Handy, Charles, *The Empty Raincoat: Making Sense of the Future* (Hutchinson, 1994)

Hardy, Francis, 'My husband's ex-lover wanted to destroy us. The tragedy is, it killed our son but has made our marriage so much stronger', *Daily Mail*, 5 July 1996

Heyland, Rob, 'How to make a drama out of a midlife crisis', *Sunday Mirror* 'You' supplement, 19 January 1997

Heyn, Dalma, *The Erotic Silence of the American Wife* (Plume, 1997)

Hite, Shere, *The Hite Report* (Macmillan, New York, 1976 & 1978)

Hollyer, Beatrice, 'When two makes a happy family', *Sunday Mirror* 'You' supplement, 9 February 1997

'How to get him back from the other woman', *Cosmopolitan*, 1982

Hunt Holman, William, 'Sad state of affair', *The Sunday Times* 'Style' supplement, 29 January 1995

Iley, Chrissey, 'A world apart', *The Sunday Times* 'Style' supplement, 14 April 1996

'Infidelity: Part 1. Special Report', *Guardian*, 11 September 1995

'Infidelity: Part 2. Special Report', *Guardian*, 12 September 1995

Jackson, Linda & Hardy, James, 'Men reduced to sex objects as women sate lust for power', *Sunday Telegraph*, 2 March 1997

Johnson, J. & Ratey, C., *Shadow Syndromes*, 1996

Kahn, Farrol, 'Flying into trouble', *The Sunday Times* 'Style' supplement, 31 August 1997

Keenan, Mary, 'Women who marry for money', *Cosmopolitan*, February 1997

Kennedy, Dominic, 'Divorcees win right to share pensions by 2000', *The Times*, 27 January 1997

Kennedy, Dominic, 'The dull truth about sex and the single woman', *The Times*, 20 March 1997

Kinsey, Alfred C. et al, *Sexual Behaviour in the Human Female* (W.B. Saunders, Philadelphia, 1953)

Kinsey, Alfred C. et al, *Sexual Behaviour in the Human Male* (W.B. Saunders, Philadelphia, 1948)

Lasson, Sally Ann, 'Dating: are you playing by the rules?', *Evening Standard*, 16 May 1996

Laurence, Jeremy, 'The way to a woman's heart is through your wallet', *The Times*, 4 April 1997

Lawrence, D.H., *Women in Love* (Penguin, 1960)

Lawson, Annette, *Adultery: An Analysis of Love & Betrayal* (Oxford University Press, 1988)

Lazarus, Richard S. & Lazarus, Bernice N., *Passion & Reason: Making Sense of Our Emotions* (OUP, 1994)

Lear, Frances, 'The second seduction', *Cosmopolitan*, July 1992

Lerner, Harriet Goldhor, *The Dance of Intimacy: A Woman's Guide to Courageous Acts of Change in Key Relationships* (Harper & Row, New York, 1989)

Lewis, Roger, 'The affair with the nanny', *The Sunday Times* 'Style' supplement, 18 February 1996

'Marriage and Divorce Statistics', Central Statistical Office, 1995

McConnell, Sara, 'Moving forward after divorce', *The Times*, 8 March 1997

McConnell, Sara, 'Pensions could cost three times mortgages', *The Times*, 15 March 1997

McGinnis, Tom, *More Than Just a Friend: The Joys and Disappointments of Extra-marital Affairs* (Prentice Hall, New Jersey, 1981)

Montefiore Morris, Sally, 'Who wins in the mistress game?', *The Sunday Times* 'Style' supplement, 25 February 1996

Montefiore Sebag, Simon, 'The ex files', *The Sunday Times* 'Style' supplement, 11 February 1996

Morris, Desmond, *The Naked Ape* (Vintage, 1967)

Mortimer, Penelope, *About Time Too* (Phoenix, 1994)

Nuki, Paul & Smith, David, 'House prices are predicted to double over next 10 years', *The Sunday Times*, 16 March 1997

Norwood, Robin, *Women Who Love Too Much* (Arrow Books, 1986)

'Our changing hearts', *Time* Magazine, 1994

Patterson, Chandra, 'Why not? (Would you love a married man?)', *Essence*, September 1989

Pinter, Harold, *Betrayal* (Eyre Methuen, 1978)

Pittman, Frank, *Private Lies: Infidelities and the Betrayal of Intimacy* (Norton, 1990)

Peele, Stanton & Brodsky, *Love and Addiction* (Taplinger, 1995)

'Planning for Social Change', Henley Centre, 1996

'Population Trends', Central Statistical Office, 1996

Pratt, Kevin, 'Hidden price of extended illness', *The Sunday Times*, 4 February 1996

'predatory woman, The', *The Sunday Times* 'Style' supplement, 26 January 1997

'Pre-family lifestyles', Mintel 1996

Priest, Jacqueline, *Families Outside Marriage*, 2nd ed. (Jordan Publishing, 1993)

Purnell, Sonia, 'Divorcees who live in dread of getting old', *The Sunday Mirror*, March 1997

Ratey, John J. & Johnson, Catherine, *Shadow Syndromes* (Bantam Press, 1997)

Reibstein, Janet & Richards, Martin, *Sexual Arrangements: Marriage, Monogamy & Affairs* (William Heinemann, 1992)

Reid, Sue, 'Caught in the net', *The Sunday Times* 'Style' supplement, 11 February 1996

Rice, Rebecca, 'Fidelity: how important can it be?', *Cosmopolitan*, March 1995

Richardson, Laurel, *The New Other Woman: Contemporary Single Women in Affairs with Married Men* (Free Press, New York, 1985)

Ridley, Matt, *The Red Queen: Sex and the Evolution of Human Nature* (Penguin, 1994)

Rubin, Zick, 'Measurement of Romantic Love', Journal of Personality & Social Psychology, 16(2), 265–73

'Sex, marriage and divorce', Christianity Today, 1992

Sissons, Saskia, 'The mistress hunter', Marie Claire, October 1996

Smith, David, 'There's no investment as safe as houses', The Sunday Times, 16 March 1997

Smith, Tom W., Attitudes Towards Sexual Permissiveness: Trends, Correlates and Behavioural Connections (National Opinion Research Center, University of Chicago, 1992)

'Social Focus on Women', Central Statistical Office, 1995

'Social Trends', Central Statistical Office, 1996

Sokolow, Bienvenida, 'Confessions of a courtesan', Daily Mail, 24 June 1996

Sokolow, Bienvenida, 'Confessions of a very modern mistress', Daily Mail, 25 June 1996

Sokolow, Bienvenida, The Making of a Modern Mistress (Smith & Gryphon, 1996)

Stoppard, Tom, The Real Thing (Faber 1982)

Summers, Diana, 'Changing face of Britain: Marriage is waning, divorce booming and "empty nesters" may be a myth', Financial Times, 23 August 1995

Sumrall, Amber Coverdale, ed., Breaking Up is Hard to Do (The Crossing Press Freedom, USA, 1994)

Talati, Smita, 'Couple should take future into account', The Sunday Times, 16 March 1997

Thomson, Alice, 'Peers defend right to play their part in running Britain', The Times, 8 February 1996

Timmins, Nicholas, 'Women set to make up 46% of workforce', Financial Times, 30 January 1997

Truss, Lynne, Making the Cat Laugh (Hamish Hamilton, 1995)

Walsh, Anthony, The Science of Love, (Prometheus Books, 1997)

Wark, Penny, 'Resolutely single-minded?', The Sunday Times 'Style' supplement, 25 February 1996

Wilkinson, Helen, Howard, Melanie et al., Tomorrow's Women (Demos, 1997)

Wright, Robert, The Moral Animal (Abacus, 1996)